T0081451

A pastor once said he needed only t[...]
church: one on sex, one on the end tim[...]
sex in the end times. David Lamb here covers all the bases on the subject
of sex in the Old Testament, in a sensible, down-to-earth, well-informed
way. He writes as a biblical scholar who knows about real life, and he
shows he can bring the Bible and our own sexual lives together. His book
would be a great textbook for at least one of those classes.

> —**John Goldingay,** David Allan Hubbard Professor
> of Old Testament, Fuller Theological Seminary

Every once in a while a book comes out that compels us to consider
subjects the Bible raises but the church tends to neglect. *Prostitutes and
Polygamists* is more than a good read. It is an expose of sexual issues the
Bible doesn't avoid that are as real and destructive today as in ancient
times. Thank you David Lamb for shedding light on these important
issues, for probing these taboo texts, and for calling Christians to engage
on behalf of the vulnerable and wounded.

> —**Carolyn Custis James,** author, *Malestrom:
> Manhood Swept into the Currents of a Changing World*

In our sexually obsessed culture, David Lamb provides a timely and honest discussion about sex in the Bible — the good, the bad, and the R-rated.
Confronting our ugliest moments, he invites us to encounter the radical
beauty of God's love for all.

> —**Tom Lin,** InterVarsity Vice President and Director of Urbana;
> Lausanne Movement International Deputy Director

Sex is a gift from God, but often it feels like a curse. We are all broken people
because of our rebellion, and thus we struggle with sexuality. David Lamb
has given us a book that acknowledges just how bad we are. Indeed, we are
worse than we think we are. But then he reminds us through this brilliant
look at biblical stories of brokenness just how big God's grace is toward us.
Once you start reading this book, you won't be able to put it down.

> —**Tremper Longman III,** Robert H. Gundry Professor
> of Biblical Studies, Westmont College

I regularly use Dave Lamb's *God Behaving Badly* when teaching the Old Testament to college students. Given the centrality of sexuality to human experience and the challenges for modern readers in engaging the Old Testament about these issues, I am thrilled that Lamb has provided another valuable resource to the church.

—**Lindsay Olesberg,** Scripture Engagement Director,
InterVarsity Christian Fellowship/USA

Most steer away from the awkward stories in the Bible. Not David Lamb. He jumps us into the toughest parts of the Bible with honesty, grit, courage, and even humor. He makes me want to read the Old Testament with new eyes.

—**Doug Schaupp,** Associate National Director of Evangelism,
InterVarsity Christian Fellowship

With unblinking and sharp eye, David Lamb delves into provocative topics like sex, marriage, and polygamy with humor. A helpful resource for serious learners of all types!

—**Nikki Toyama-Szeto,** editor, *Partnering with the Global Church*

The only books I read these days are those which throw fresh light on Scripture or challenge traditional presuppositions. Top-rated Old Testament scholar David Lamb has done both in this thought-provoking book.

—**Frank Viola,** author, *From Eternity to Here* and *Jesus: A Theography* (with Leonard Sweet), *frankviola.org*

Sometimes it takes humor to take something really seriously. And David Lamb takes sex very seriously indeed, and his humor only underlines that. For this is serious biblical ethics, tackling laws and stories in the Old Testament that many either avoid with embarrassment or exploit with venom as a way of attacking Christian understanding of sex and marriage. Lamb combines careful scholarly reading of the biblical texts with a light and engaging touch, while pointing the way for pastors, churches, and the rest of us to be a lot more biblical, discerning, and Christlike in what (and who) we love, and a lot more robustly honest and informed about what the Bible actually says (and doesn't say) about sex.

—**Christopher J. H. Wright,** Langham Partnership;
author, *Old Testament Ethics for the People of God*

PROSTITUTES AND POLYGAMISTS

PROSTITUTES AND POLYGAMISTS

A Look at Love, Old Testament Style

DAVID T. LAMB

ZONDERVAN

Prostitutes and Polygamists
Copyright © 2015 by David T. Lamb

This title is also available as a Zondervan ebook. Visit www.zondervan.com/ebooks.
This title is also available in a Zondervan audio edition. Visit www.zondervan.fm.

Requests for information should be addressed to:
Zondervan, 3900 *Sparks Dr. SE, Grand Rapids, Michigan 49546*

Library of Congress Cataloging-in-Publication Data

Lamb, David T. (David Trout), 1962–
    Prostitutes and polygamists : a look at love, Old Testament style / David T. Lamb.
      pages   cm
    Includes bibliographical references and index.
    ISBN 978-0-310-51847-1 (softcover)
    1. Sex – Biblical teaching. 2. Sex crimes – Religious aspects – Christianity. 3. Bible. Old
Testament – Criticism, interpretation, etc. I. Title.
    BS680.S5L355 2015
    220.8'3067 – dc23   2015000742

All Scripture quotations, unless otherwise indicated, are taken from *The Holy Bible, English Standard Version*, copyright © 2001 by Crossway Bibles, a division of Good News Publishers. Used by permission. All rights reserved.

Scripture quotations marked NIV are taken from The Holy Bible, *New International Version®, NIV®.* Copyright © 1973, 1978, 1984, 2011 by Biblica, Inc.® Used by permission. All rights reserved worldwide.

Scripture quotations marked NRSV are from the *New Revised Standard Version of the Bible*, copyright © 1989 by the Division of Christian Education of the National Council of Churches of Christ in the United States of America, and are used by permission. All rights reserved.

Scripture quotations marked NASB are from the *New American Standard Bible*, Copyright © 1960, 1962, 1963, 1968, 1971, 1972, 1973, 1975, 1977, 1995 by The Lockman Foundation. Used by permission.

Any Internet addresses (websites, blogs, etc.) and telephone numbers in this book are offered as a resource. They are not intended in any way to be or imply an endorsement by Zondervan, nor does Zondervan vouch for the content of these sites and numbers for the life of this book.

All rights reserved. No part of this publication may be reproduced, stored in a retrieval system, or transmitted in any form or by any means – electronic, mechanical, photocopy, recording, or any other – except for brief quotations in printed reviews, without the prior permission of the publisher.

Cover design: *CAMPANA DESIGN*
Cover photography: *iStockPhoto*
Interior design: *Dan Dingman*

Printed in the United States of America

---

15 16 17 18 19 20 21 22 23 24 25 /DCI/ 20 19 18 17 16 15 14 13 12 11 10 9 8 7 6 5 4 3 2 1

To Nathan and Noah

CONTENTS

ACKNOWLEDGMENTS

One afternoon thirty years ago, I picked up a hitchhiker in Palo Alto, California, who introduced herself to me as Domino. After a few questions, she let me know that she was working. I thought, "How can you be working while you're hitchhiking?" I asked, "What kind of job do you have?" She then informed me she was a "lady of the daytime." I gave her no business that day but prayed for her and told her that Jesus is a friend of sinners and prostitutes. At the end of our interaction, she told me her name was Sandy. I wish I had been familiar with the material in this book before I met her so that I could have also told her about Tamar, Rahab, Abraham, and David, all those heroes of the Old Testament who, despite serious sexual issues, were redeemed by the grace of God. To begin this section of the book, I need to acknowledge Sandy, the hitchhiker prostitute, who opened my eyes to a world I had been shielded from.

Most of the other people I'll acknowledge here for shaping this book are not prostitutes, or polygamists for that matter.

Many friends and colleagues at Biblical Theological Seminary have supported me in various ways, encouraging, listening, and editing. Todd Mangum allowed me to arrange my teaching load to give me time to write. It has been my delight to teach much of this material to BTS students, and they in return have taught me and blessed me greatly. Phil Monroe, Carolyn Custis James, and Diane Langberg offered wise counsel, improving my writing and helping me solve a variety of problems.

My editor Katya Covrett was enthusiastic about the project, improved the writing along the way, and offered wisdom and perspective, particularly at several key points when I was confused about how to get past significant roadblocks. Jesse Hillman listened carefully, took my comments seriously regarding cover design, and was willing to tag me as a polygamist. I am confident that many other people at Zondervan, whom I haven't met yet, will be helpful to me after these acknowledgments have been written.

At church, my Sunday school class, the Gathering, was willing to put up with the wacky Bible professor who wanted to talk about sex in the Old Testament as we looked at the dark side of the story of Abraham, Sarah, and Hagar. Our small group (Bob, Deb, Mike, Sue, Don, Maggie, Yinka, and Iyabo) carried me through a difficult and painful time and, unlike my family, were very eager to discuss prostitutes and polygamists. One of the pastors at my church, Jeff Supp, helped me at several points in the process, sharing with me written materials, as well as his own insights about how parents can discuss sex with their children.

Within the context of InterVarsity Christian Fellowship, I learned not only how to study Scripture, but also not to ignore the difficult bits, so I'd like to thank my many IV friends, particularly the ones I mention in this book (Sharon, Jesse, Rich, Gary, Katherine, and Bill).

My dad continues to be my biggest supporter. I hope I can manage to be as encouraging to my sons as he has been to me. Dad, I couldn't have written this book without you (and Mom).

After I've been slaving away at the office, writing about prostitutes and polygamists, Tig is the only member of my family who races to the door to greet me. Instead of telling me to add another Oxford comma, he just licks my face.

Shannon is my love, my partner, my proofreader, my scuba diving buddy, my 'ezer kenegdo, the bone of my bone and flesh of my flesh. I love being a parent with her, and while I dread the next stage (empty-nest), I console myself that I'll be going through it with her.

My two sons, Nathan and Noah, tolerated many dinner conversations about rapists and adulterers. ("Do normal families talk about polygamy as much as we do?") For my first book, they were distractions; for the second, they were research assistants; for this one, they were editors. I am immensely proud of them (even when they beat me in ping-pong). They will always be the arrows in my quiver.

CHAPTER 1

HUMANS BEHAVING BADLY

The Worst Sin You've Ever Committed

"Turn to the person next to you and confess the worst sin you've ever committed."[1] I thought, "You're kidding, right?" The conference speaker seemed to read my mind, responding verbally to my unspoken question: "I'm serious. Worst sin ever. Go."

I was a twenty-seven-year-old unmarried InterVarsity staff worker, and on my immediate left was an eighteen-year-old first-year female student. I was at the end of the row; there was no one on my right I could turn to for escape. I didn't normally sit next to freshmen women (and never would again), since I didn't want to do anything that could be construed as flirting (sharing deep sexual sins might be construed as flirtatious), but I had come late to the meeting, and there had been only a few open seats. We didn't normally begin meetings in this manner, and if I had known what the speaker was going to do, I would have gone to a different section of the room and stood. For most people

---

1. I wanted to start each chapter of this book with an obscure, yet surprisingly relevant, quote in Latin. Unfortunately, I know no Latin nor any obscure, yet relevant, quotes.

there, the first sin that came to mind was probably in the sexual realm, and I was in the majority. It was an extraordinarily awkward moment for all of us, so much so for me personally that twenty-four years later I still have a vivid memory of how I felt and what I was thinking.

But we shouldn't have been shocked by the fact that people sin, since most of the people present were Christians, and therefore, we had already declared that we sin. The Bible gives us no excuse for being reluctant to talk about sexual sins, since it has no problem sharing the worst sins ever committed by some of the holiest people who have ever lived, and many of those sins are of a sexual nature. I was uncomfortable sharing my worst sin with one other person, but that's nothing compared with having my worst sin published in the bestselling book of all time. Why is talking about sin, and sexual sins in particular, so uncomfortable? For many of us, our discomfort talking about sex begins at a young age in our families.

Love, American Style

"You may freely watch of every program in the early evening, but of the program of the knowledge of love and sex, you shall not watch, for in the day you watch of it, you'll be grounded."

This was the prohibition spoken by the Lamb parents to the Lamb children in 1972. (I may have paraphrased their actual words.) Before computers, Blu-ray, DVRs, DVDs, Netflix, live streaming, and YouTube, visual home entertainment was just television. No cable, just NBC, CBS, and ABC. A family VCR was still a decade in the future. On Friday nights starting at 7:00 p.m. (Central Time in Ames, Iowa), we three boys typically watched ABC's *The Brady Bunch*, *The Partridge Family*, *Room 222*, and *The Odd Couple*. Then the TV was turned off, and I headed to bed shortly afterward. (I was ten.)

The forbidden program? *Love, American Style*. It came on at 9:00. Each episode included unconnected stories of love, sex, and romance that our parents deemed unworthy for our young eyes.

Strangely, the parental prohibition just made the desire to watch it stronger. We thought it would be good to watch and a delight to the eyes. On those rare occasions when we figured out a way to see it, our eyes were opened. We realized the show wasn't all that good, only occasionally funny, often lousy, always silly. Silly, because love, American style, was quirky. But as quirky as love is in the US, in the Old Testament, it was even quirkier.

Love, Old Testament Style

Love, Old Testament style, was weird, bizarre, and often unholy. The book of Genesis makes it clear what the ideal was — one man, one woman, together, forever — but often for the people of God, the ideal was not the reality. The Old Testament doesn't just talk about sex but includes many incidents of what would now be considered deviant sexual behavior. Love may be "a many splendored thing," but in the Old Testament, it went beyond splendored to bizarre. And strangely, the authors didn't have any qualms about reporting these weird sexual practices in a book that was meant to be read to children (Deut. 4:9–10; 6:7, 20; 11:19; 32:46; Josh. 8:35). For most readers, the "love" stories of the Old Testament raise a lot of questions.

Judah praised his daughter-in-law Tamar for being righteous after he realized she tricked him into having sex with her for money. *In Judah's day was it considered a good thing to have a daughter-in-law as a prostitute?*

Jacob, who gave his new name, Israel, to the nation, had several wives. Solomon, who was considered the wisest man ever to live, had several hundred. *Was it considered wise back then to be a polygamist?*

While visiting the city of Gibeah, a Levite's concubine was forced to have sex with the men of the town throughout the night until she was dead (Judges 19). *What were the biblical authors thinking when they decided to include this horrific story? "Hey, the Bible needs a few more gruesome stories of gang rape"?*

The book of 1 Kings seems to have forgotten that David had sex with Uriah's wife Bathsheba — and then killed Uriah to cover it up — when it declared that David kept God's commandments completely and did only what was right (1 Kings 14:8). *Since when is it righteous to commit murder and adultery?*

"Did Cain really marry his sister?" If you haven't asked that question, you were probably embarrassed the first time a clever junior higher in the Sunday school class you were teaching did. Incest isn't just for modern royal families; ancient biblical families also engaged in it.

In terms of sexual deviancy, the Old Testament is worse than an episode of *Arrested Development*.[2] Why does the Bible talk so much about polygamy, prostitution, rape, adultery, and incest? Because the Bible talks about real humans, and often humans behave badly. The Bible doesn't ignore bizarre sexual behavior, but parents and churches often do.

"What's a Foreskin?"

My mother passed away in August 2012, so now I can write a book on sex. Seriously, I really miss my mom and have committed to tell stories about her as much as possible as I continue to grieve her death. But it would have been awkward for her to read a book I wrote about sex, even sex in the Bible. Not only were my parents uncomfortable with my brothers and I watching shows that talk about sex, but they were also uncomfortable talking to us about sex, which was fine with us.

We were not alone. When it comes to sex, parents and children have one thing in common: they desperately want to avoid the topic. My teenage sons are not excited that I'm working on this book right now. My friend Sharon posted this message on Facebook recently: "Well, my six-year-old came back from a long time of reading the Bible (the Lego Bible) in her room and said, 'Mom, first of all, what's a foreskin? And what does it mean to lay with someone?'"[3] Awkward,

---

2. An American TV show on Fox from 2003–2006 about a highly dysfunctional family and their business in Southern California. I'll talk more about the show soon.

3. It may be called the Lego Bible, but for copyright purposes, it goes by *The Brick*

yes, but clever of Sharon's daughter to realize that Mom was the person she should ask what those confusing words mean.

Children's Bibles are usually no help, because they conveniently skip over things like David's adultery (or rape?) and murder. (The book of 1 Chronicles, curiously, does the same thing; 1 Chron. 20:1–2; 2 Sam. 11:1; 12:26.) I would like to see a children's Bible that is a bit more true to the text in the area of sex and sexuality. (Despite using small plastic bricks to communicate its message, the Lego Bible doesn't really fit into the genre of Kid Lit.)

The parental aversion to sexual discussions means there's often a deafening silence on the subject. It's not just six-year-olds asking about foreskins. In the Old Testament classes I teach, youths and adults frequently ask me about biblical attitudes toward polygamy, prostitution, rape, adultery, incest, and homosexuality. (Hopefully it's not because they're thinking, "Hey, this guy looks like he *knows* a lot about prostitution and incest.") Who will speak into the silence and answer their questions? Unfortunately, often it's not the church.

"Maximum Sex"

Parents avoid the subject of sex, and Christians in general do the same. Most churches avoid talking about sex. Can you imagine a sermon series on sex in Scripture? What about a Sunday school class on polygamy? How about a discussion of the incest laws (Leviticus 18) in your small group Bible study?

My senior year in high school (still in Ames, Iowa), I took four of my closest friends to Hilton Coliseum to hear Josh McDowell, a popular speaker with Campus Crusade for Christ (shortened simply to "Cru" in 2011). I couldn't get my friends to come to church with me, but they were willing to hear Josh. Why? The title of his talk was "Maximum Sex." Unfortunately, I don't remember as many sermons as I should, but more than thirty years later, I still remember his main point. He

---

Bible: A New Spin on the Old Testament by Brendan Powell Smith (New York: Skyhorse, 2011).

explained that sex as God designed it (one man, one woman, together, forever) results in maximum joy, pleasure, and intimacy.

I realize that more churches are gradually focusing attention on some of these sexual topics, but when Christians do talk about sex, it's still big news. As I was working on this chapter, the CBS news website highlighted a church outside of Houston promoting its new sermon series, "Love Sex."[4] It made national headlines because it's still so unusual. (I'm sure attendance will go up during the series for this church.)

Josh McDowell's talk and the Houston church sermon series are the exceptions that prove the rule. Christians don't talk about sex enough, which made the willingness of this church and this speaker so shockingly unusual and headline-grabbing. People apparently really want to hear what the church has to say about sex. (And provocative titles always help.)

When the church does teach on sex and sexuality, it tends to focus exclusively on the ideal — one man, one woman, together, forever — which is good, but not sufficient, since the ideal is often not the reality. If someone in the church gets divorced or commits adultery, we don't know how to react, because people rarely talk about these issues. Many times when someone is raped or sexually abused (even sometimes within church buildings), a tragic situation is made worse when the incident is ignored, avoided, or covered up. While parents and churches may avoid the subject of sex, our culture doesn't.

Arrested Development and the Old Testament

If the church is sexually avoidant, our culture is sexually obsessive. And it seems to be becoming more severe. When I was growing up, programs addressing the topic of sex, like *Love, American Style*, were the exception; now they are the norm.

---

4. Jessica Hartogs, "Texas Church Surprises with 'Love Sex' Sermon Series," *CBS News.com*, September 4, 2013, *http://www.cbsnews.com/8301-201_162-57601309/texas-church-surprises-with-love-sex-sermon-series/*.

There's the obvious: *Sex and the City, Modern Family*, and *Big Love* (the story of a polygamous family in — wait for it — Utah). Perhaps the best example is *Arrested Development*, where in any given episode, teenaged George Michael and his cousin Maeby might flirt with incest; his grandmother Lucille might sleep with her husband George's brother Oscar (so, polyandrous, incestuous adultery); Maeby's mother, Lindsay, might unsuccessfully attempt an affair; and George Michael's father, Michael (played by Jason Bateman), might hire a woman he thinks is his sister, but who's really a prostitute (played by Jason Bateman's actual sister, Justine). It's hilarious and tragic. Prostitution, adultery, and incest, just like the Old Testament.

When the church whispers about sex and the culture yells about it, whose voice is going to be heard? And parents wonder what happened to their children. The church needs to talk about sex more — not just the ideal but also the reality. And the great thing is if parents or the church want some good material to teach from, all they have to do is open their Bibles. Granted, it's confusing sometimes, but understanding will come through examination, not avoidance.

An R-Rated Bible?

The Bible talks about sex all the time. It's not uncomfortable with the subject. A few pages ago, I mentioned the Lego Bible, which goes by the name of *The Brick Testament*, an online retelling of the Bible using Legos.[5] While one might think that Legos + Bible = Children's Bible, before you bookmark the website on your child's computer, you need to know the whole story.

The website comes with content warnings, and each story has appropriate labels: N = nudity; S = Sexual Content; V = Violence; C = Cursing. For example, the story of the creation of the humans and their eating of the fruit (Gen. 2:4–3:24) has all four warning labels: N, S, V, and C. When the text speaks about the man and the woman becoming one flesh (Gen. 2:24), according to the *Brick Testament* they

---

5. Here's the website: *http://www.thebricktestament.com/home.html.*

are actually consummating their relationship, certainly a reasonable assumption (see the next chapter of this book).[6] Naked Lego Man is on top of Naked Lego Woman, and they are both smiling. (And so am I, while wondering whether I should feel guilty for voyeuristically experiencing their moment of intimacy. Fortunately, anatomical adjustments have not been made to the Lego creatures.) In the *Brick Testament*, the book of Genesis is divided into forty sections, and more than half (twenty-two) of the sections have an S or an N rating. If you were to translate those into film ratings, the book of Genesis would get an overall rating of R, or perhaps worse. *I told you to wait on that bookmark.*

The books of Leviticus and Deuteronomy have chapters devoted to legislation regarding sexual relations (Leviticus 18; Deuteronomy 22). Numbers 25 narrates how Israelite-Moabite sex led to idolatry. In addition to the gang rape of the Levite's concubine, Judges records Samson's failed first marriage, his encounters with a prostitute, and his sexual relationship with Delilah (Judges 14–16). The climax of Ruth is when she climbs into bed with Boaz in the middle of the night and uncovers his "feet" (Ruth 3:4–8). I'll let you decide how to interpret Esther's reaching out and touching the tip of the king's extended scepter (Est. 5:2). The book of First Samuel begins with the polygamist father of Samuel, then proceeds to inform readers that the priestly sons of Eli were sleeping with prostitutes at the entrance of the tabernacle (1 Sam. 1:2; 2:22). The most common image for idolatry in the prophetic books is adultery/prostitution. (There are too many texts to list, but here are a few: Isa. 1:21; Jeremiah 2–3; Ezekiel 16, 23; Hosea 1.) The entire Song of Songs (or Song of Solomon) is about sex. I'm going to stop now, but I could keep going.

Parents and churches have plenty of options to choose from to start gently raising their voice in this area. If we were merely to follow the biblical example and talk about sex as often as Scripture does, we would be forced to break our vow of sexual silence.

---

6. See *http://www.thebricktestament.com/genesis/the_garden_of_eden/14_gn02_24 .html.* The book version, *The Brick Bible*, is a bit less racy; they are just holding hands, not consummating their relationship (p. 17).

Humans Behaving Badly

A recent *Time* magazine article on the sexual antics of New York politicians Eliot Spitzer and Anthony Weiner was titled "Men Behaving Badly."[7] (Aren't you tired of the formula "X Behaving Badly"? The expression is overused.) While it seems like every few weeks a politician or church leader is caught up in a new sexual scandal, things weren't that different in Old Testament times. Some things never change.

As we've already seen, sections of the Old Testament could be renamed "Humans Behaving Badly," because both godly men (Jacob, Judah, and David) and godly women (Tamar, Rahab, and Ruth) appear to be involved in unholy sexual behavior.[8] But that's not the only type of negative behavior I want to focus on here. When parents and churches blatantly ignore significant sections of the Bible that describe non-ideal sexual behavior, they are also behaving badly.

While many of these sexual stories may not seem suitable for family dinner conversation, if the divinely inspired biblical authors thought the stories were worthy of being recorded for posterity, then we shouldn't ignore them. Obviously, parents and churches need to use discernment regarding what is appropriate for their audiences, but if the result is avoidance of biblical texts mentioning sex, then our standards need to be loosened.

Paul states that "all Scripture is inspired by God and profitable for teaching" (2 Tim. 3:16 NASB), and when Paul said "Scripture," he was referring to the Old Testament. If we never teach about the polygamists, prostitutes, rapists, adulterers, and Sodomites[9] of the

---

7. Eliza Gray, "Men Behaving Badly," *Time* (July 26, 2013). The web version was titled "Weiner and Spitzer: Will Voters Reward Bad Behavior at the Polls?" (See *http:// swampland.time.com/2013/07/25/men-behaving-badly/.*) John Goldingay wrote a book about the books of 1 and 2 Samuel with the title *Men Behaving Badly* (Carlisle, UK: Paternoster, 2000) before the formula "X Behaving Badly" had become common.
8. While the sexual deeds of Judah, David, and Rahab were clearly unholy, the sexual deeds of Jacob, Tamar, and Ruth were not. We will discuss all of these individuals in the following chapters.
9. I capitalize *Sodomites* because I'm referring to the residents of Sodom. (See chapter 7 for a longer discussion.)

Old Testament, then we don't really believe Paul, at least not when it comes to these "love" stories. However, if we do teach about them, we will profit, according to Paul, and part of that profit will involve fewer people falling into these types of sinful behaviors. In order to be humans who don't behave badly, we must teach about humans who do behave badly, and as we do, we will learn profound things about the behavior of our God.

God Behaving Graciously

Another reason to examine these stories of messed-up heroes of the faith is that they have powerful lessons to teach us. When we ignore their stories, we deny the power of God's grace, because as humans' bad behavior abounds, God's gracious behavior abounds even more (a loose paraphrase of Rom. 5:20). Time and time again we see that when humans behave badly, God behaves graciously.

How does God show grace? In three ways. First, God graciously records the stories of people with messed-up sex lives in Scripture to help others learn about sin, grace, and healing. Imagine if the worst sexual sin that you committed were recorded in the bestselling book of all time. How would that feel? Ouch. Yes, well, that's what the Bible does. That doesn't sound like grace. Ironically, however, it is. As people throughout history have read these painful stories about sexual sin, they get a sense of God at work and of God forgiving. "Making lemonade out of lemons" is too trite, but that's the idea. Did these people know their stories were recorded? We can't be sure, but many of them had to know, since they were the ones telling the stories originally. Painful stories serve a redemptive purpose to bless the originators as well as later hearers and readers.

Second, God graciously invites people with sexual issues to be part of his mission to accomplish his purposes in the world. This is a huge theme of the whole Bible — that God isn't limited by human sin, that he can work through polygamists like Jacob, prostitutes like Rahab, and adulterers like David. The church today includes many who know that their sexual background isn't ideal. For them, God's desire to work through broken vessels is a great message of hope.

Third, God graciously loves people, even ones who behave badly sexually. He doesn't only record their stories and invite them into his mission, but he forgives their sins and heals their sexual brokenness. Recording, inviting, and forgiving are all part of God's great, gracious love toward all of us. But we see this perhaps most powerfully in these Old Testament "love" stories. Love, Old Testament style, is not just about weird human behavior, but it's also about incomprehensible divine behavior, love toward undeserving people who screwed up and yet are still included and healed. This style of "love" story doesn't conclude at the end of the First Testament but is continued in a surprising way at the beginning of the Second Testament, so each chapter of this book will conclude by looking at how Jesus addresses these topics and loves people who behave badly.

Seventeen Verses

The New Testament begins by summarizing the Old Testament in seventeen verses. How does one take a story that is told over the course of twenty-three thousand verses and squish it into just seventeen verses?[10] By focusing on one thing. For Matthew the focus is on the production of children, which, in case you didn't know, comes from having sex.

The first seventeen verses of the New Testament record the genealogy of Jesus (Matt. 1:1–17), and while all genealogies speak of procreation and, therefore, sex implicitly, Matthew's version highlights sex in two other ways.

First, while Luke's genealogy is more euphemistic about sex (Luke 3:23–38), Matthew's genealogy addresses the subject more directly. Luke, working backward from Jesus to Adam, uses the word *of* to

---

10. The usual figure given for Old Testament verses in Christian Bibles is 23,145, but this sum can vary depending on several factors; see "Chapters and Verses of the Bible," *http://en.wikipedia.org/wiki/Chapters_and_verses_of_the_Bible.*

signify the relationship between father and son.[11] However, Matthew, working forward from Abraham to Jesus, speaks of each father "fathering" his son, using the Greek verb *gennaō*. Unfortunately, most modern translations take the verb *gennaō* and make it into a noun in the expression "the father of …" While the verb *gennaō* is used forty times in these seventeen verses in the Greek, English translations have few or no verbs. This nounification of a strong verb dramatically changes the meaning, as these fathers transform from being active to passive. It appears the English translators were uncomfortable, like the parents we discussed earlier, with speaking of sex in a less euphemistic manner.

The King James Version renders *gennaō* nicely as the verb "begat," but people don't beget anymore, so no contemporary English translations use verbs like the KJV does. The best verbal equivalent in English is "fathered." The fathering being spoken of here isn't raising the child but merely producing the child. And while the mother's role in reproduction goes way past the initial sexual act leading to conception, from a physical standpoint sex is the only thing a father does to "father" a child. To support this interpretation, the word *gennaō* is translated a few verses later as "conceived," speaking of the fetus of Jesus conceived in Mary by the Holy Spirit (Matt. 1:20). Conception happens only after sex (although not in Jesus' case).

Jesus' Prostitute Grandmothers

Matthew's genealogy emphasizes sex in a second way. While Luke's genealogy mentions no mothers, Matthew's mentions five (Tamar, Rahab, Ruth, Bathsheba, and Mary), all of whom have some type of sexual problem. The first four all have another thing in common: they all appear to be non-Israelites. Tamar and Rahab were Canaanites, Ruth was a Moabitess, and Bathsheba was perhaps a Hittite, like her husband, Uriah. The one thing shared by all five of these women is a scandalous sexual history.

---

11. Luke merely uses the genitive, masculine singular form of the definite article (*tou*), thus literally "Jacob of Isaac of Abraham of Terah" (Luke 3:34).

Tamar dressed up as a prostitute to seduce her father-in-law, Judah (Genesis 38), so she appears to be guilty of prostitution and incest at the same time, a two-for-one. Rahab also was a prostitute, but unlike Tamar's one-time foray, she pursued it as a career, which meant she served as an experienced host for the two Israelite spies visiting Jericho (Joshua 2). Ruth was a Moabite widow who sneaked up to Boaz in the middle of the night and laid down next to him (Ruth 3:4–8). Bathsheba, who is unnamed in Matthew ("the wife of Uriah"), was guilty of adultery with, or was possibly the victim of rape by, King David. Mary became pregnant outside of wedlock and then gave birth to what would have appeared to those around her to be an illegitimate son.

Both in the Old Testament and in the literature of the ancient Near East, the vast majority of genealogies were like Luke's and omitted mothers, so Matthew's maternal inclusions must have been intentional. But why these? One might expect that the first mothers to be included would be the more respectable ones like Sarah, Rebekah, and Leah, who were wives of patriarchs (Abraham, Isaac, and Jacob), or perhaps some of the lesser-known ones like Jehoaddin, Jecoliah, or Jerusha, who were wives of three righteous kings (Joash, Amaziah, and Uzziah).[12]

However, Matthew's genealogy lists none of these, just the five mothers with problematic sexual backgrounds. Thus, the New Testament begins by highlighting not only Jesus' foreign ancestry but also his scandalous ancestry. Two of Jesus' grandmothers were prostitutes. Shouldn't that sort of information have been swept under the rug?

That type of tidying up the family tree might happen today, because parents and churches typically ignore this aspect of Jesus' story as part of a bigger cover-up of the sexually scandalous nature of Scripture. But that's not what the Bible does. Both the Old Testament and the New

---

12. I assume you can find the references for Sarah and Abraham, for Rebekah and Isaac, and for Leah and Jacob in the book of Genesis on your own, but since the three I've mentioned are harder to find, here are the references for Jehoaddin and Joash, for Jecoliah and Amaziah, and for Jerusha and Uzziah: 2 Kings 14:2; 15:2; 15:33.

Testament boldly raise the topic of sex. The Old Testament introduces the subject of sex right away with the first command to "be fruitful and multiply." It's therefore not surprising that the New Testament continues that tradition by summarizing the Old Testament sexually with the genealogy of Jesus.[13] We will discuss these scandalous women later, Tamar and Rahab with the prostitutes (see chapter 4), Bathsheba in the context of her relationship with David (see chapter 5), Ruth briefly in chapters 3 and 6, and Mary in the epilogue. As we look at the sexual scandals of these women, we'll discover a few surprises. And it's not just with Jesus' grandmothers where we find this sexual emphasis.

Jesus' Polygamist Grandfathers

I mention the sexually scandalous foreign women in Jesus' genealogy in my book *God Behaving Badly*, as have numerous other recent authors,[14] but the sexual scandals of two of Jesus' grandfathers are often overlooked. It would appear that many Christians feel more comfortable pointing out sexual problems for women than for men.

Forty of Jesus' fathers are named in Matthew's initial genealogy, but two stand out: Abraham and David. The first verse of the New Testament declares that Jesus was a son of David and a son of Abraham. Most of Jesus' ancestors are mentioned twice (first as a son, then as a father), but Abraham is mentioned three times (since the genealogy starts with him, he should have been mentioned only once) and David five times.

Unlike the included mothers, the Old Testament provides a lot of information about these two men, but in addition to being ancestors of

---

13. The connection between Matthew and Genesis is made more pronounced when one looks at the first Greek words *biblos geneseōs*, which are often translated as "book of the genealogy" of Jesus Christ (Matt. 1:1), but *geneseōs* is a feminine genitive form of the main noun *genesis*. In the Hebrew tradition, Genesis was called *bere'shit*, literally "in the beginning," from the first Hebrew word (Gen. 1:1).

14. David Lamb, *God Behaving Badly: Is the God of the Old Testament Angry, Sexist, and Racist?* (Downers Grove, Ill.: InterVarsity, 2011), 86–87. See also Rachel Held Evans, *A Year of Biblical Womanhood* (Nashville: Thomas Nelson, 2012), 46.

Jesus, they have one other thing in common: sexual issues. Curiously, among all the men with sexual problems and sins whom this book focuses on, only two appear prominently in multiple chapters of the book: Abraham and David. Both were polygamists and both were involved with sexual scandals. Abraham, the father not only of Jesus but also of faith itself (Rom. 4:9–16), appears in every chapter, sometimes positively but more often negatively. Shocking, perhaps, but only because we tend to ignore this part of the biblical story. Hopefully, this book is a small step in the other direction, taking the biblical theme of sexuality seriously since it reveals God behaving graciously toward humans behaving badly.

Hebrews 11 and Acts 7

One of the reasons we ignore the sexually deviant behavior in the Old Testament, as well as Jesus' sexually scandalous genealogy in Matthew 1, is that we often have a Hebrews 11 perspective on the Old Testament. The so-called Hall of Faith of Hebrews 11 recounts the faithful examples of Old Testament saints, such as the patriarch Abraham, who offered to sacrifice his son, Isaac; such as Moses, who identified with the people of God; and such as the people of Israel, who passed through the Red Sea (Heb. 11:17, 25, 29).

We look for heroes to emulate in the pages of the First Testament, and when we find them, we base a Sunday school curriculum or a vacation Bible school theme on their exemplary lives: "Dare to Be a Daniel!" So when we encounter prostitutes and polygamists in these Old Testament narratives, we don't know what to do. Themes like "Dare to Be a Polygamist!" or "Dare to Be a Prostitute!" don't work well for a VBS theme. (I dare you to try those.) The Hebrews 11 model of faithful examples is certainly a biblically valid one, because all believers, including the heroes in the Hall of Faith, were looking forward to the author and perfecter of our faith, Jesus (Heb. 12:2).

But the Hebrews 11 model for teaching from the Old Testament isn't the only legitimate one. In Acts 7, Stephen gives a speech to the high priest and the Jewish council summarizing the deeds of his ancestors, and he has a different take on his predecessors. He doesn't find saints to emulate; rather he finds sinners to learn from, such as the patriarchs who sold their brother Joseph into slavery; such as Moses who killed the Egyptian; and such as the people of Israel who made the golden calf (Acts 7:9, 24, 41).

Hebrews' Hall of Faith and Acts' speech of Stephen are both viable models for how to use the Old Testament in teaching. Sometimes we focus on positive examples (Hebrews 11), sometimes on negative examples (Acts 7).

In two consecutive chapters of Psalms, we see another example of these alternative methodologies for summarizing narratives. Psalm 105 focuses positively on God's faithfulness to his people, who apparently do no wrong. Psalm 106 focuses negatively on the sinfulness of his people, who apparently do no right. We can use both of these biblical models, the positive (Hebrews 11 and Psalm 105), as well as the negative (Acts 7 and Psalm 106), when we study and teach the Old Testament. This book is an attempt not to ignore the problematic sexual sections of the Old Testament but to discuss them so that we can teach them. Read on and dare not to be — but to learn from — polygamists and prostitutes, adulterers and rapists, incesters and Sodomites.

A Word about Humor

Before winding down this introductory chapter, I need to make a comment about humor. Humor is a serious business. Some people thought that *God Behaving Badly* was flippant. If you felt that way, I apologize. But how many books have you read about the Old Testament that erred in the direction of too much humor? (Some people said *God Behaving Badly* had no humor at all. I resemble that remark.) My guess is that few to none err in that direction, and for all the complaints I heard about my supposed irreverence, there were more affirmations about my wacky sense of humor.

I use humor to serve at least three purposes. First, humor helps us deal with pain. Many of these topics of sexual behavior do not seem conducive to humor, particularly rape and prostitution. But weeping and laughing are both effective ways to deal with grief and tragedy, as people who've been to a good memorial service know. In August of 2012, I wept and laughed during my mother's memorial service. During the summer of 2013, comedienne Tig Notaro became an overnight sensation as she spoke candidly, and hilariously, about the death of her mother, a near-fatal infection, a painful breakup, and a diagnosis of breast cancer.[15] After Notaro's mother's death, the hospital sent Notaro a survey: "How was her stay?" Notaro replied, "Not great." Humor with pain.

Second, humor helps us speak the truth. George Bernard Shaw reportedly said, "If you are going to tell people the truth, you better make them laugh; otherwise they'll kill you." Humor lowers people's guard to allow them to hear truth that they might otherwise have disagreed with and reacted negatively to. Humor can establish trust between people, making it easier for a relationship to "handle the truth."

Third, humor keeps us humble. The target of much of my humor is myself. My family would say there's a lot of material there to work with. Jokes that are most likely to get people into trouble are ones that make others the brunt of the joke. Jesus tells us that those who humble themselves will be exalted (Luke 18:14). Humor is a great way to be humble.

Speaking of humor, though, let's switch to the topic of parental sex.

Your Parents Had Sex

Despite a generational aversion to visiting the topic of the birds and the bees, the one thing that most strongly connects parents to children is sex. You may not be aware of this, but your parents had sex to create you.[16] This bond, which most parents and post-puberty children

---

15. See Lily Rothman's article about Tig Notaro, "Comedian Tig Notaro Looks Back — And Forward," in *Time*, July 11, 2013: *http://entertainment.time.com/2013/07/11/comedian-tig-notaro-looks-back-and-forward/*.

16. For adoptive children, change this to, "Your birth parents had sex . . ."

are actually aware of, should make it natural for cross-generational discussions about sex to take place. And yet it doesn't happen often or soon enough.

A 2009 article in *Time* magazine argues that parents and children need to talk about sex earlier and more frequently, since 40 percent of adolescents had sex before talking to their parents about it.[17] Both Planned Parenthood and Focus on the Family agree that parents and children need to talk about sex more.[18] There are many good reasons for more cross-generational sex talks. According to the research, children actually do want to learn about sex from parents. The more parents discuss sex with their children, the more likely the children are to take on their parents' sexual values. Children who talk to parents about sex are more likely to delay sexual activity. Teens often name parents as the biggest influence on their attitudes toward sex.

I clearly remember the last time my dad talked to me about sex. Nineteen years after the prohibition to watch *Love, American Style*, I was sitting with my dad on a park bench (back in Ames, Iowa). I had just married Shannon two weeks earlier in California, a few blocks from Disneyland, where her parents lived. After our recently completed tennis match (Dad and I remember the result differently), Dad told me he wanted to give me some advice about sex.

I need to interrupt my story with a little background about my family. My older sister, Cheryl, was from my mom's first marriage, and my younger brother, Wayne, was adopted. So my older brother, Rich, and I are the only two biological children from both Mom and Dad.

Dad starts by telling me about his sexual relationship with Mom. I was shocked. "You guys had sex?"

He smiled and said, "Twice."

The gist of his advice was that I needed to be a servant in my sexual

---

17. Alice Park, "Parents' Sex Talk with Kids: Too Little, Too Late," *Time*, December 7, 2009, *http://content.time.com/time/health/article/0,8599,1945759,00.html*.
18. Planned Parenthood, "Talking to Kids about Sex and Sexuality," *http://www .plannedparenthood.org/parents/talking-kids-about-sex-sexuality-37962.htm*; Focus on the Family, "Talking about Sex and Puberty," *http://www.focusonthefamily.com/ parenting/sexuality/talking_about_sex.aspx*.

relationship with Shannon, that I needed to focus more on her needs than on my own. Neither father nor son felt comfortable during the conversation, but I deeply appreciated his willingness to talk about an awkward subject. I still vividly remember what he said. The fact that he spoke to me about sex made an impact in my life to this day. I have tried to follow his advice. Shannon and I have two sons, so, just like my parents, we've also had sex twice.

CHAPTER 2

HUSBANDS AND WIVES

The Smoochy Professor

It was Saturday, and I was teaching Genesis to a class of counseling students. Our day of teaching had begun early at 8:30 in the morning and was to last until 4:30 in the afternoon. After a long week of work, instead of relaxing with family and friends, we were spending our Saturday sitting in a classroom. Many of the students had to drive more than an hour each way to attend the class. Sessions like these make for a long day for both student and professor. I take it as a personal challenge to keep students engaged, awake, and alert. I'm basically exercising on stage for eight hours. At 5:00 p.m., I return home to collapse into a blob on the couch.

This particular Saturday we were discussing the creation of humans, specifically how the first man greeted the first woman in Genesis 2:23. I was in room 25, which gives the instructor, but not the students, a great view out the door into a long hallway past the academic office and the admissions office. As I looked out the door, I saw someone walking toward our classroom. I'm nearsighted, and since I don't normally wear glasses while teaching, I couldn't tell who the person was initially, but once I recognized the approaching individual, I exclaimed, "Bone of my bones and flesh of my flesh!"

A woman the students had never seen burst into the room. I swept her into my arms and we smooched. (I am now known by the young daughter of one of the students as "the smoochy professor." I've been called worse.) The class erupted in applause. The mysterious woman was, of course, my wife, Shannon, who was dropping off coffee cake for the class. I wasn't expecting her, but the timing was perfect, divinely arranged not only to keep my students awake for a long day in class but also to illustrate the passion a husband should have for his wife. Just as God brought Shannon and me together that day, he orchestrated the first meeting between a man and a woman.

We Are Godlike

Before moving into the problematic realms of sexual behavior, such as polygamy and prostitution, in the following chapters, we first need to talk about what sex should look like. To understand God's view of sex and sexuality, the best place to begin is "in the beginning."[1] So we'll take a close look at the first few chapters of Genesis, since they describe the ideal for marriage.

On the sixth day of creation, after making plants, fish, birds, and land animals, God finally creates humans.[2]

> Then God said, "Let **us** make man in **our** *image*, after our *likeness*. And let **them** have dominion over the fish of the sea and over the birds of the heavens and over the livestock and over all the earth and over every creeping thing that creeps on the earth."

---

1. See also my discussions of Genesis 1–3 in *God Behaving Badly*, 49–60, 116–20.
2. The seven "days" of creation do not need to be understood as a literal twenty-four-hour period of time. The Hebrew word used for "day," *yôm*, has three distinct meanings in Genesis 1–2. First, a twenty-four-hour period of time, as suggested by the expression "evening and morning" (Gen. 1:5). Second, daytime, as God calls the light *yôm*, "day" (Gen. 1:5), roughly twelve hours. Third, a weeklong period of creation, as the text speaks of the "day" (*yôm*), which was really a week, that Yahweh made the heavens and the earth (Gen. 2:4; see also Gen. 1:1, 8, 10), so 168 hours (= seven times twenty-four).

> So God created man in his own *image*,
>   in the *image* of God he created **him**;
>   male and female he created **them**.
>
> — Genesis 1:26–27

In this first appearance of humans in the Bible, the text informs us that God made them as sexual beings, both male and female. The words used here for "male" (*zakar*) and "female" (*neqebah*) are used as a pair in five other places in the book of Genesis (Gen. 5:2; 6:19; 7:3, 9, 16). What does it mean for the humans to be male and female? In these verses, this meaning is connected to the image of God. (Theologians like to use the term *imago dei*; apparently the Latin sounds more spiritual.)

It's shocking that God made humans in his image. Paul tells us that all humans "fall short of the glory of God" (Rom. 3:23), and Calvinists remind us of our "total depravity." And yet, Genesis informs us that we are divinely human. Men and women bear his image. We are, therefore, godlike. These two verses emphasize this divine connection four times, twice in each verse ("our image," "our likeness," "his image," and "the image of God").

What does it mean to be made in God's image? The rest of the Bible fills out the picture of what God is like, but so far in Genesis, all God does is create, which has obvious implications for the realm of human sexuality. But first we need to talk about pronouns.

Talking about Pronouns

God first uses plural pronouns for himself — "Let **us** make man in **our** image"[3] — but when God actually gets around to doing the creating, the text uses a singular: "So God created man in **his** own image." I'll avoid the sticky theological issue of whether the Trinity is being suggested by the plural forms in 1:26[4] and just make the observation

---

3. While Hebrew has pronouns (either attached to another word as a suffix, or independent), often the appropriate pronoun is merely implied by the verbal form, which is the case here with "Let us."
4. For the various possibilities of interpreting these plural divine pronouns, see Gordon J. Wenham, *Genesis 1–15* (Waco, Tex.: Word, 1987), 27–28.

that in two consecutive verses the text uses both plural ("us" and "our") and singular ("his") pronouns for God.

The switch from first person ("our") to third person ("his") makes sense, since God himself is speaking in verse 26 and he is being spoken about in verse 27, but the switch from plural to singular is confusing. And what makes it even weirder is the parallel nature of the phrases:

- "Let **us** make man in **our** image ..."
- "God created man in **his** image ..."

Everything is parallel in these two lines except the pronouns, as if the text is trying to confuse us.

Is God singular or plural? Yes. We may never fully comprehend what it means that God is both individual and corporate, but that's what the usage of these pronouns suggests here. This dual aspect of God is one of the first things we discover about God in the Bible. The rest of Scripture will help us flesh this concept out.

Now look at what the text does in the rest of verse 27.

> In the image of God he created **him**;
> male and female he created **them**.

Humans are both "him" and "them." The text of verse 27 describes the humans in the same way verse 26 describes God, using both singular ("him") and plural ("them") pronouns.

Are humans singular or plural? Yes. At least in respect to plural-singular pronoun usage, humans and God are similar, which shouldn't be surprising since God made humans in his image. What does that mean? From these verses we see that God and humans are somehow both individual and corporate beings. From Genesis 1 it is difficult to say much about God's corporate nature,[5] but for the humans, we see that their corporateness involves their sexual nature as male and female.

---

5. The breath, wind, or spirit (*rûaḥ*) of God appears in Genesis 1:2, and according to John 1:1–2, Jesus as the "word," *logos*, was around from the beginning, but from the perspective of Genesis 1, we're going to have to wait awhile for Jesus to physically appear in the Bible.

But if humans are both male and female, why do English translations use the word "man" here? The Hebrew word behind "man" is *'adam*, which can mean "a specific person named Adam," "a generic man," or "humankind in general," as the NRSV renders it here. We know the word here is referring not to Adam or to a specific man but to humankind generally because the *'adam* here incorporates both genders. The text is speaking not of a single androgynous being but of humanity as a corporate entity consisting of males and females.

These two verses tell us several things about the first humans. First, God created humans as sexual beings, male and female. At this point we don't get any details about differences between the two genders, but it is important to note that sexuality is mentioned at the very beginning of human creation.

Second, humans have two distinct natures, but also a unified nature as humans. They are male and female, and the text repeatedly uses plural pronouns ("them"). But they are also spoken of singularly as *'adam*, understood as "humankind" and with a singular pronoun ("him"). In short, the two are also one.

Have a Lot of Sex

The freshly made humans don't have anything to do yet, so God gives them a task:

> And God blessed them. And God said to them, "Be fruitful and multiply and fill the earth and subdue it."
> — Genesis 1:28a

God is creative, so he wants his image-bearers to create as well, and for them this will involve things like tilling the garden and naming the animals, as we'll see in Genesis 2, but it will also involve bearing fruit, like it did for the plants and animals, as we saw in Genesis 1. In case you're not clear on this yet, to bear fruit, they will need to have sex. That's just how it happens. For more details, ask your parents.

How much sex are we talking about? Enough to fill the earth. Presumably, they won't need to accomplish this task by themselves, but it still sounds like a lot (pre-Viagra). God's first words to the humans are essentially, "Have a lot of sex!" In terms of the earth-filling mandate, I think we can check that one off our to-do list, but that doesn't mean God wants us to stop having sex. Love, Old Testament style, involved sex (within a marriage).

God created sex, and we know that he's excited about this part of his creation because not only does his first command to the humans involve sex but so does his first command to other living creatures. God wants the plants (Gen. 1:11–12, 29), the animals (1:22), and now the humans all to bear fruit (1:28). Because all of God's creation — plants, animals, and humans — are sexually active, fruit will be borne and creation will re-create itself.

We see here in the first divine-human interaction that God is not afraid of discussing the birds and the bees with the birds and the bees, as well as with the humans. He doesn't put off the subject like many parents do, but he brings it up during his first interaction with his young "kids." Perhaps we should follow his example?

God "Likes" His Creation

As God creates everything, he keeps giving his creation a thumbs-up (Gen. 1:1–31). He makes light and says, "That's good," basically clicking on the "like" button. Next, earth and sea — again, "like." Plants, "like." Sun and moon, "like." Fish and birds, "like." Animals, "like." God likes the "like" button. He'd have lots of friends on Facebook.

God likes his creation. The Hebrew word for "good," *tov*, appears seven times in the first chapter of the Bible when God stops each day to evaluate positively the new things he's made. (He skips day 2, but does it twice on days 3 and 6; Gen. 1:4, 10, 12, 18, 21, 25, 31.) The pattern is consistent with the first six evaluations, but something different happens with the seventh. Instead of just *tov*, God says *tov me'od* — it was "very good." It would be like a double "like" on Facebook (although when you click a second time on "like" on Facebook, it toggles off, so not like that).

What gets God so excited? The humans, in his image, male and female, bearing fruit. I told you God is excited about sex — although it might be better to say he wants his image, in the form of his human image-bearers, to be spread throughout the planet, but he knows that will happen only with a male and a female coming together.

Not Good

After God takes a break to rest on the seventh day (Gen. 2:2–3), the text takes a break and backs up to retell the story of creation, with a different twist. The first creation account (Gen. 1:1–2:4a) is poetic and formulaic and has a global perspective. The second account (Gen. 2:4b–25) is personal and narrative and has a garden perspective. The first account calls God just "God," in Hebrew *elohim*, but the second account calls God *yhwh elohim*, or as it usually is translated into English, "the LORD God." (When the Hebrew text calls God *yhwh*, I will refer to him as Yahweh, and when it calls him *elohim*, I will refer to him as God.)[6] The usage of God's name Yahweh in the second narrative makes it more personal.

Yahweh first makes the man (*'adam*) out of the ground and then places him in a beautiful garden where Yahweh has provided for the man abundantly with every kind of plant and tree, as well as four plentiful rivers (the Pishon, the Gihon, the Tigris, and the Euphrates) and extravagant precious stones, jewels, and, my personal favorite, bdellium — the *b* is not silent. Then something shocking happens. Something is *lo tov*, "not good." God doesn't "like" part of his creation.

> Then the LORD God said, "It is **not good** [*lo tov*] that the man should be alone; I will make him a ***helper fit for him*** [*'ezer kenegdo*]." Now out of the ground the LORD God had formed every beast of the field and every bird of the heavens and brought them to the man to see what he would call them. And whatever the man called every living creature,

---

6. Most English Bibles translate *yhwh* as "the LORD", but I prefer "YHWH" or "Yahweh." The name "Jehovah" is essentially a misspelling of God's personal name.

that was its name. <u>The man</u> gave names to all livestock and to the birds of the heavens and to every beast of the field. But for <u>Adam</u> [or "the man"] there was not found a helper fit for him ['*ezer kenegdo*].

—Genesis 2:18–20

Notice that the text here refers to him not as "Adam" but as "the man," so I will do the same.[7] If you're a bit confused, since the order of creation is different in this second creation account, read this note.[8]

Not Even the Pink Fairy Armadillo?

There are two weird things about these three verses. First, it's weird that God made something not good. It was not good for the man to be alone. Something was not perfect at the beginning of God's creation. And why does the text call that to our attention? Doesn't it make God look bad? It seems like God didn't really know what he was doing, kind of like me when I'm putting together an IKEA bookshelf with the little hex tool, and I realize I've left off a shelf or two or three. Didn't God realize ahead of time that this would be a problem? He should have measured twice so he could cut once. (I always measure once, cut twice.)

Second, it's weird that God thought a zoo was going to provide companionship for the man. (Although, a man's best friend *is* a dog …) I can imagine God asking the man while he is naming the animals, "Pink Fairy Armadillo, Duck-Billed Platypus, Proboscis Monkey,

---

7. I won't go into the details, but the ESV's translation of "Adam" in Genesis 2:20b follows the pointing of the Hebrew Masoretic text, but the NRSV's translation of "the man" makes more sense in the context since the man is not clearly called "Adam" until Genesis 4:25.

8. In the first creation account, plants come first, then animals, and finally humans together on the sixth day, but in this second account, the man comes first, then plants and animals, and finally the woman. The first account and the second account emphasize different aspects of creation and aren't obsessed with the order of events as we are today. The divinely inspired authors of Scripture surely knew that there were tensions between these two versions, but they apparently didn't care.

Woolly Mammoth, Sucker-Footed Bat, Pygmy Marmoset …[9] Hey, man, any of these animals going to work for you?"

"Nope."

You might think, since God made the man (*'adam*) from the ground (*'adamah*), that these other ground creatures might do the trick and keep the man company, but alas, to no avail. It's still not good for the man to be alone. It looks like God will need to resort to Plan B.[10]

Plan B

Fortunately, Plan B works.

> So the LORD God caused a deep sleep to fall upon <u>the man</u>, and while he slept took one of his ribs and closed up its place with flesh. And the rib that the LORD God had taken from <u>the man</u> he made into a woman and brought her to <u>the man</u>. Then <u>the man</u> said,
>
> > "This at last is bone of my bones
> >   and flesh of my flesh;
> > she shall be called Woman [*ishah*],
> >   because she was taken out of Man [*ish*]."
> > —Genesis 2:21–23

While the man is under general anesthesia, Yahweh performs the first surgery, a ribectomy, on the man, who apparently checked the wrong box on his driver's license. ("If you are willing to have spare parts harvested while you are still living, check here.") Yahweh, who can work wonders with limited ingredients, makes the rib into a woman, whom he then brings to the man.

I've come out of general anesthesia several times and have always felt groggy for a while. (They don't let you drive for twenty-four hours.)

---

9. These are all real animals. Google them. If you like mythical creatures, the KJV has unicorns (Num. 23:22; 24:8; Job 39:9–10; Ps. 29:6; 92:10) and dragons (Neh. 2:13; Ps. 91:13; Isa. 27:1; 51:9; Jer. 51:34; Ezek. 29:3).

10. If my speaking of God having a Plan B concerns you, wait a few pages.

I imagine recovery from a lost rib could take several days, and yet this guy is so interested in what God is bringing to him that grogginess and pain aren't part of the equation.

Since the text doesn't tell us what he named the animals, his words to the woman are the first human words recorded in the Bible. The text isn't interested in telling us how he learned to speak, just what he says. These first words spoken by the man and heard by the woman are foundational for understanding the relationship between the sexes.

Ish and Ishah

Some Christians think that the fact that the man called her "woman" means that he has authority over her before the sin of the eating of the fruit (Gen. 3:6).[11] Curiously, some of the scholars who believe that the man's naming of the woman is important don't think it's important to follow the text, because they refer to her not as "the woman," the name given to her by the man and used sixteen times in this section (Gen. 2:22, 23, 24, 25; 3:1, 2, 4, 6, 8, 12, 13(2), 15, 16, 17, 21) but as "Eve," the name that the man gives her after they eat of the fruit (Gen. 3:20).[12] While God does name the things he creates in the first creation narrative, the male authority argument doesn't make sense in this context for three reasons.

First, the story of the creation of the woman is not about the establishment of submission but is about the quest for a companion. The passage begins by stating that it isn't good for the man to be alone (Gen. 2:18), and it ends with the man finally finding a suitable companion (Gen. 2:23). Yahweh brings the animals to the man "to see what he would call them" — not to establish the man's authority over them but to determine whether any are deemed worthy partners, a process which allows the man to discover his need for one. In the previous creation account, God has already established that both the man and

---

11. See Wayne Grudem, *Evangelical Feminism and Biblical Truth* (Sisters, Ore.: Multnomah, 2004), 31–33.
12. Ibid.

the woman have authority over the rest of creation (Gen. 1:28). As the man names the animals, no suitable partner is found, so the companion-quest continues. The man is put to sleep, the rib is removed, he is awakened, and she is brought to him. Notice, God never commands the man to name the woman; the man just spontaneously cries out. Based on his exclamation, we know the quest is over; a suitable helper has finally been found.

Second, the name given to the woman emphasizes not authority but equality. He calls her *ishah*, which can mean "woman" or "wife" and is merely the feminine form of the word used for the man, *ish*, which can similarly mean "man" or "husband."[13] His declaration isn't, "Submit to me, woman," but, "Let's be husband and wife." By his choice of a name, the man signals not that the hierarchy has been established but that the problem has been solved. He calls her the name that is most like his own (*ish, ishah*) to emphasize their equality in different form as male and female. When I greet Shannon, "Hi, wife," I'm not trying to put her in her place but signaling her unique role as the one person on the planet I can call "wife," the only woman I've committed my life to. I smile when she responds, "Hi, husband."

Third, the context is describing Yahweh's search for a "helper as partner"[14] for the lonely guy and not for a second in command. While the word *help* may have negative hierarchical connotations today involving slaves, servants, or secretaries (think of the book and film *The Help*[15] about the relationship between black servants who "help" white housewives in Mississippi in the 1960s), that is not the case in the Bible. The Hebrew word rendered as "helper" in English translations is *'ezer*, and in the Bible, the one primarily doing the helping is God. With only one exception, every other time when *'ezer* is used in the Pentateuch, God is the helper (Gen. 49:25; Exod. 18:4; Deut. 33:7, 26, 29). The woman here is going to act in a godlike manner for the man

---

13. William Webb makes a similar argument in *Slaves, Women, and Homosexuals* (Downers Grove, Ill.: InterVarsity, 2001), 116–17.

14. The NRSV renders the Hebrew (*'ezer kenegdo*) in Genesis 2:18, 20 as "helper as his partner."

15. Kathryn Stockett, *The Help* (New York: Putnam, 2009); the film came out in 2011.

as his divinely appointed helper, but lest we think she is supposed to be his superior like God is for us, the text qualifies her role. The Hebrew word modifying *'ezer* is *kenegdo*, which could be translated literally into three English words: "like opposite him." The companion is similar, but different, like a mirror image. BDB, the classic Hebrew-English dictionary, defines this exact form in the context of Genesis 2:18 as a help "equal and adequate" for the man.[16] Old Testament scholar Derek Kidner describes her as "wholly his partner and counterpart."[17]

Not the Pink Fairy Armadillo, the Duck-Billed Platypus, the Proboscis Monkey, the Woolly Mammoth, the Sucker-Footed Bat, the Pygmy Marmoset, and not even man's best friend, the dog, provide the sought after *'ezer kenegdo* for the man (2:20). Only the woman provides the perfect *'ezer kenegdo*, the *ishah* for the *ish*. When it wasn't good for me to be alone, God provided me with the perfect *'ezer kenegdo*.

Shannon, My *'ezer*

It was 4:30 in the morning. I was in the middle of my first-ever panic attack. I was in the bathroom unable to sleep. If you're not familiar with them, panic attacks involve serious stress and incontrollable anxiety. I cried out, "God, help me. God, help me."

To provide some background to my crisis, the previous year had been a busy one for me, involving too much yelling as a youth soccer and basketball coach and too much speaking at churches and campus fellowships, which resulted in vocal cord damage. I had to cancel speaking engagements. In the midst of voice problems, serious stress was added to my life when my mom and my brother-in-law died and my dad was hospitalized.

When I finally went to see a doctor, he thought stomach reflux was causing my voice problems, so he prescribed a battery of medicines (Prilosec, Zantac, and a steroid). I don't often take many meds, so I'm

---

16. See F. Brown, S. Driver, and C. Briggs (BDB), *The Brown-Driver-Briggs Hebrew and English Lexicon* (1906; Peabody, Mass.: Hendrickson, 1997), 617.

17. Derek Kidner, *Genesis* (Downers Grove, Ill.: InterVarsity, 1967), 65.

sensitive to them, and this particular cocktail gave me headaches and made the reflux worse. I started having sleep problems, which began a downward spiral in my health. I was getting only a few hours of sleep a night, and I was losing half a pound every day. All of which leads back to the 4:30 a.m. bathroom panic attack and my cry for help.

As an answer to prayer, my wife, Shannon, came into the bathroom. Looking sleepy and rubbing her eyes, she asked, "Are you okay?"

I replied, "No. I'm miserable. I can't sleep. For the first time in my life, I understand why people commit suicide."

Just having her with me made things a little bit better. Then she spoke words of comfort for me, she read verses from the Bible for me, and she prayed prayers of blessing for me — until I could sleep. Over the next few months, God eventually healed my reflux, my vocal cords, my sleeplessness and panic attacks, but through this dark period of my life, Shannon was my *'ezer* in a way I had never needed her before. It was not good for me to be alone.

The First Love Poem

Back to Genesis 2, the main point of the man's declaration to the woman has nothing to do with authority and everything to do with romance, and mixing those two is usually a really bad idea. Notice that his declaration, the very first human words, are also a poem ("bone of my bone, flesh of my flesh"), and not just any kind of poem but a love poem, singing the praises of his wife, his muse. Perhaps not a Shakespearean sonnet, but love poetry was different back then. (Read the Song of Solomon.) Love, Old Testament style, involved poetry.

Imagine the scene. She's just been created and doesn't know what's happening or who this naked guy in front of her is, and now she realizes she's naked too. Well, they don't know they're naked yet; that comes later (Gen. 3:7). But that doesn't change the fact that they are in fact naked. Might she feel a bit vulnerable? Yes. But then he publicly exclaims his connection to her (same bone, same flesh) and boldly proposes to her by declaring that they should be husband and wife.

I'm not particularly romantic (ask my wife), but even I can see the romance here.

In case you're not convinced yet, look at how he begins, captured well in the ESV and NRSV as, "Now at last." Why "at last"? He's been waiting for a long time. The text tells us the man named every living creature, every bird of the air, and every animal of the field. How long would that take? Even if he were to ignore the insects, the process could take days. I don't think this passage should be taken strictly literally, but categorizing the class, order, family, genus, and species of all the animals in creation could still take awhile. The zoological option, Plan A, didn't work because it resulted in no 'ezer kenegdo, but Plan B works so beautifully that after an extensive interviewing process, the position is finally filled, the man realizes his quest is over, and he declares, "At last!"

While the text doesn't make it explicit, it suggests that God knew from the beginning exactly what he was doing. Plan B wasn't an afterthought but was intended all along by God. Yahweh was orchestrating events to create longing and anticipation, so that when the 'ezer kenegdo finally appeared, the man was ecstatic and burst into a love song.

For most married couples, waiting is part of the process — waiting to date, to get engaged, to be wed, and to be intimate. While no one likes to wait, it's a big theme of Scripture. In Genesis we see Abraham waiting for an heir, Jacob waiting for a wife, and Joseph waiting for a dream. Ideally, waiting forces us to be more dependent on God, just as the man was in Genesis 2. When we choose not to wait, not to trust, and to rush the process, the consequences are severe, even with repentance and forgiveness, as we see in Genesis 3.

The One Becomes Two; the Two Become One

After the man's poem, the narrator adds a comment, familiar in weddings, but still strange.

> Therefore a man shall leave his father and his mother
> and hold fast to his wife, and they shall become one flesh.
> And the man and his wife were both naked and were not
> ashamed.
>
> — Genesis 2:24–25

So the man is supposed to leave his father and mother and cleave to his wife. At this point a question should slap you in the face: who are these supposed parents? The first man and woman don't have any. The man came from the ground and the woman from a rib.

We must not be talking about just Ground Boy and Rib Girl anymore. The narrator is broadening the lesson to apply not just to this first union but to all future unions by making the point that the new relationship of husband and wife takes priority over the old relationship of parent and child. Once again the text isn't afraid of broaching the subject of sex, mentioning it here both in the idea of becoming one flesh and in the idea of being naked and unashamed.

God takes the man he's created and makes another, a woman, as *'ezer kenegdo* for him; then he brings them together to become one flesh. In step one, the one becomes two; in step two, the two become one.

Prior to the man's love song, the humans are passive in the process and Yahweh is active. Yahweh notices the problem of aloneness, forms the animals from the ground, brings them to the man, acknowledges the lack of a solution, anesthetizes the man, operates on the man, and brings the two of them together. The man sleeps and is silent. It's a beautiful picture of this human's dependence on his God. If the people in Scripture (as well as people today) had been able to follow the example of this first man, who trusted his God to provide the perfect companion for him, many of the sexual problems discussed later in this book would have disappeared.

Before looking at those problems, we need to clearly state the importance of this passage. In Genesis 2:24 we find the clearest expression of the biblical ideal for marriage: one man, one woman, together, forever. This ideal is supported by other texts scattered throughout the Bible (Exod. 20:14, 17; Deut. 5:18, 21; 24:5; Ps. 128; Prov. 5:15–20; Eccl. 9:9;

Matt. 19:5; Mark 10:6–9; 1 Cor. 6:16; Eph. 5:31). Each of these texts directly or indirectly refers back to Genesis as the foundation for a biblical understanding of marriage.

Shame, Pain, and Rule

The love story of Genesis 2 takes a tragic turn in Genesis 3. All of the sexual problems that we'll discuss in this book can be traced to the moment when the first humans decided not to trust God and ate the forbidden fruit. The consequences of this act of disobedience were catastrophic, affecting all aspects of human experience. But for this book, we'll focus on three sexual consequences.

1. Shame and Nakedness

> Then the eyes of both were opened, and they knew that they were naked. And they sewed fig leaves together and made themselves loincloths.
>
> — Genesis 3:7

Like the bad dream of waking up at school naked, the man and the woman instantly realize they are wearing their birthday suits, so they quickly throw together a green ensemble from the fig leaves nearby. Despite the fact that Yahweh later provides them with hip Flintstonesque animal skins (Gen. 3:21), they are doomed forever to be portrayed in paintings and comics wearing those gauche fig leaves. (Eve, of course, also covers up on top with long hair.)

While we don't know exactly what their nakedness is meant to represent (be skeptical of interpreters who do), at the basic level, nothing had previously separated them from each other physically or sexually. They were without shame (Gen. 2:25). Now, however, their nakedness and shame lead them to hide from God and cover up their exposed sexuality with clothes. As a result, their natural intimacy and mutual vulnerability suffer.

2. Pain and Desire

After asking the man and the woman about what had happened and listening to their excuses, Yahweh explains the negative effects, sometimes called the curses, but perhaps more accurately called the consequences. I'll focus on the woman's because it affects male-female relationships most significantly.

To the woman he said,

> "I will surely multiply your pain in childbearing;
> in pain you shall bring forth children.
> Your desire shall be for your husband,
> and he shall rule over you."
>
> — Genesis 3:16

Earlier in the text, God told them to multiply fruit; now he's telling Eve that he is going to multiply pain in the process of bearing fruit. They are still supposed to fill the earth, but it's going to be less pleasant. "No pain, no gain." One might think this new bit of information would provide a wife with a serious disincentive to becoming one flesh with her husband, but Yahweh adds that despite the pain, she'll still desire him.

When our first son, Nathan, was born, Shannon almost died. We were living in West Philadelphia, and Shannon went into labor on the hottest day in Philadelphia's history (July 15, 1995). Nathan was content in the womb, and like his father, he can be stubborn, so he didn't want to come out, extending Shannon's labor for thirty-six hours, causing her to become dehydrated. She gave birth at a world-class hospital, the Hospital of the University of Pennsylvania, but it was still scary because she lost so much blood. As she lay in her bed, she looked like a ghost. She also gave birth naturally, with no painkillers.

Afterward, she told me, "I'm never doing that again." I was hoping for another child, so I was disappointed, but what could I say? "It couldn't have been that bad"? Or perhaps, "No pain, no gain"? Fortunately, I said nothing. Over the course of the next year, Shannon changed her mind, and twenty-one months later, with less pain, Nathan gained a younger brother, Noah.

While children are definitely worth it, birth hurts. At least that's what I hear from friends who are moms, and I assume they're not making it up. The fall really screwed things up. But it gets worse.

3. Husbands Rule

Instead of the way God designed it, husband and wife as *'ezer kenegdo*, as mutual helping partners, who together have authority over the plant and animal kingdoms, now the husband rules the wife. ("He shall rule over you.") This consequence of sin has implications in all aspects of the male-female relationship. We see many of these implications in the Old Testament and will discuss them in later chapters on polygamy, prostitution, rape, adultery, and incest. The negative impact of sin in the sexual realm is obviously still present today. Fortunately, there is a glimmer of hope, even among these consequences, with a reference to a future head-crushing defeat of a descendant of the serpent by a descendant of the woman (Gen. 3:15), which seems to look forward hopefully toward the New Testament.

Dust, Stars, and Sand

But before making a big jump forward to Jesus, let's make a smaller jump forward to Abraham, who was a descendant of Adam and Eve, as well as Noah and his son Shem.[18] The first patriarch will appear in a negative light in several later chapters, but here I want to begin with the positive, the ways Abraham trusted God in the area of sex.

> Now the LORD said to Abram, "**Go** from your country and your kindred and your father's house to the land that I will show you. And I will make of you a great nation, and I will **bless** you and make your name great, so that you will be a **blessing**. I will bless those who **bless** you, and him who dishonors you I will curse, and in you all the families of the earth shall be **blessed**."

---

18. God changes his name from Abram to Abraham in Genesis 17:5, but I'll just refer to him as Abraham.

> So Abram **went**, as the LORD had told him, and Lot
> **went** with him. Abram was seventy-five years old when he
> **departed** from Haran.
>
> — Genesis 12:1–4

Because of Abraham's radical obedience to the call to leave his country and kindred behind in Haran, Yahweh promises to bless him and all the families of the earth and to make him into a great nation (Gen. 12:1–3). But to become a nation, you need children, which leads to the big problem. Abraham and his wife, Sarah, have none. No being fruitful, no multiplying (perhaps a good thing if you're not into times tables). Assuming that they know about the birds and the bees, and that they've been doing everything necessary to make babies, they still have a problem. Abraham is now seventy-five and Sarah is sixty-five — not exactly spring chickens.

People today might think, "No kids, no big deal." In 2013, *Time* ran a cover story on how many couples are choosing a life without children in order to "have it all."[19] But in Abraham and Sarah's day, "having it all" meant children and a family. Descendants meant security for the future; childlessness was a source of embarrassment and shame.

To make matters worse, God keeps promising to Abraham that his descendants will be numerous, like the dust of the earth, the stars of the heaven, and the sand of the sea (Gen. 13:16; 15:5; 22:17). Wherever Abraham looks, down to the dust of the ground, out to the sand of the sea, and up to the stars of the sky, he's reminded by nature of God's promise to give him many descendants.

God gives Abraham nice images, but he still doesn't have any children. So Abraham complains bitterly to his God: "O Lord GOD [Yahweh], what will you give me, for I continue childless, and the heir of my house is Eliezer of Damascus? … You have given me no offspring" (Gen. 15:2–3). God listens and takes Abraham's complaint seriously, but as is often the case with God, instead of fixing the situation right away, he makes it worse.

---

19. Lauren Sandler, "The Childfree Life: When Having It All Means Not Having Children," *Time*, August 12, 2013, *http://www.time.com/time/cov ers/0,16641,20130812,00.html.*

Cut Off Part of Your Penis

Yahweh appears again to Abraham after Hagar gives birth to Ishmael (see chapter 3) and ironically changes his name from "Exalted Father" (Abram) to "Father of a Multitude" (Abraham),[20] to which the patriarch must have been thinking, "But Sarah and I still don't have our own son." Then Yahweh tells him that the sign of the covenant will be circumcision, which might not seem too bad until you stop and think about it. When males are circumcised today, it's typically done a few days after birth with no complications, but when it's performed as an adult, it's a bit more tricky, and recovery time is much longer.

Later in Genesis, after Jacob's daughter Dinah is raped by Shechem, her brothers plot revenge by convincing the men of Shechem's city that they need to be circumcised before they and the people of Jacob can intermarry (Genesis 34). They agree, and while they are still helpless, recovering from their circumcision, they are slaughtered by Dinah's brothers (Gen. 34:25). For the Shechemites, circumcision was fatal. When I teach on the subject, I show an image from an Egyptian tomb relief of an ancient circumcision from Saqqara, and the tool used for the cutting is no surgeon's scalpel; it's a potsherd. And the circumcised Shechemites were much younger than Abraham. If I were Abraham, I would have been reluctant to say, "Here am I, LORD, circumcise me."

To be blunt, when Yahweh tells Abraham to be circumcised, he is saying, "Cut off part of your penis with a potsherd." Half of my readers are now saying, "Ouch." (The part that had to go was the foreskin, a retractable fold of skin near the tip of the penis.) When you're hoping to have a child and have been waiting decades for a son, you might think it's a bad idea to have penis surgery at age ninety-nine. Old bodies don't heal quickly. Perhaps he should have gotten a second opinion?

I don't remember my circumcision, but I do remember my vasectomy at age thirty-five. The prescription for healing involves putting an ice pack on your privates to reduce swelling. After a couple of days, I thought I was healed, but I discovered after a bit too much walking

---

20. See the discussion of Abraham's name in Wenham, *Genesis 1–15*, 252–53.

around that I still needed a few more days. Jacob's sons would have had no problem slaughtering me.

For Abraham, obeying this command would have been harder than leaving his family behind in Haran. If this procedure went wrong, it meant no more family. But when God told him to get circumcised, he also promised that Sarah would give birth to a child in a year. And at this point, Abraham believed God and trusted him completely.

Sarah did give birth to Isaac a year later, just as Yahweh had promised, and infant Isaac was circumcised ninety-nine years younger than his dad, on his eighth day (Gen. 21:1–4). Assuming it took a couple of months for Old Man Abraham to fully recover from potsherd penis surgery before he felt like being frisky with Sarah, it is likely that their first post-circumcision sexual encounter resulted in the conception of Isaac (three months + nine months = twelve months). God blesses us when we trust him with our sexuality.

Now Abraham has reminders of the covenantal promise from God in the stars of the sky, in the sand on the beach, in the dust on the ground, and in the penis in his trousers. Every time Abraham relieves himself, he is reminded of the promise that God will make him into a great nation and that all the families of the earth will be blessed through him.

Inviting Jesus to the Marriage

The most significant way God fulfills the Genesis 12 promise to bless all families of the earth is through one of Abraham's "stars." But unlike Abraham, Jesus' method of blessing involves death, not procreation. Though Jesus was a lifelong bachelor, he supported the Genesis ideal of two becoming one. (And Jesus never told anyone to cut off part of their penis — just their hand.) Jesus' support for the institution of marriage can be seen as he attends a wedding right after calling his disciples and chooses to make it the occasion of his first miracle.

> On the third day there was a wedding at Cana in Galilee,
> and the mother of Jesus was there. Jesus also was invited

to the wedding with his disciples. When the **wine** ran out, the mother of Jesus said to him, "They have no **wine**." And Jesus said to her, "Woman, what does this have to do with me? My hour has not yet come." His mother said to the servants, "Do whatever he tells you."

Now there were six stone water jars there for the Jewish rites of purification, each holding twenty or thirty gallons. Jesus said to the servants, "Fill the jars with water." And they filled them up to the brim. And he said to them, "Now draw some out and take it to the master of the feast." So they took it. When the master of the feast tasted the water now become **wine**, and did not know where it came from (though the servants who had drawn the water knew), the master of the feast called the bridegroom and said to him, "Everyone serves the good **wine** first, and when people have drunk freely, then the poor **wine**. But you have kept the good **wine** until now." This, the first of his <u>signs</u>, Jesus did at Cana in Galilee, and manifested his glory. And his disciples believed in him.

—John 2:1–11

This wedding celebration gets off to a disastrous start when they run out of wine. It would have been horribly embarrassing to the couple and their family — even worse than a church running out of coffee on Sunday morning — a lifetime of shame in a culture that values hospitality. It's a good thing the couple invited Jesus to their wedding. He is a man with a plan.

He tells the servants to fill up the six purification jars with water, twenty to thirty gallons each, then to take some to the feast-master. While Jesus' instructions would have seemed weird (he hadn't chalked up any miracles yet), the servants still obey him. At some point in the process, the water becomes wine, but the servants probably don't know it as they hold a cup to the feast-master's face. The cup would not have looked like a wine glass today, more like the ugly clay pot I baked in the school kiln in third grade. The feast-master is so impressed that he exclaims that this new batch, Chateau de Cana '30, makes the good stuff they have already finished off seem like Thunderbird.

One might conclude that since Jesus never married, he didn't approve of the institution (see also the epilogue), but this viticultural transformation, the first of his miracles, suggests otherwise. Not only that, but this significant sign signifies what type of guest Jesus is when invited not just to a wedding but into a marriage. Specifically, we learn three things about Jesus' provision from this miracle.

Jesus the Great Liquor Provider

First, Jesus provides abundantly. He supplies 120 to 180 gallons of wine to people who've already had a lot to drink. Jesus is wildly generous to this newly wedded couple from Cana, which is consistent with what we've seen about God in Genesis. God provided generously for the first humans with an abundant garden full of good things (trees, rivers, even bdellium), and he continues to do so with his divine-image bearers today. Sometimes Jesus' provision involves material or physical blessings; often it doesn't. Yet Jesus still blesses us relationally, emotionally, and spiritually as we invite him into our marriages and into our lives.

Second, Jesus provides excellently. Jesus' wine is such a great vintage it makes the good wine they served at the beginning of the feast seem nasty. As a host, Jesus isn't cheap, but extravagant. He doesn't have to spend any money (just supernatural power), but he doesn't need to make such a quality product to meet the need of the moment. Again, we see a continuity here with the story in Genesis: God notices a problem (it isn't good to be alone or without wine), then steps in to fix it in such an incredible manner that the man and the feast-master declare their ringing endorsement of the generous gift. Lest my point here be misconstrued, it's not like the wife is a commodity to be consumed like wine by the husband, but that each are meant to be a gift to the other, celebrated and delighted in, like great wine ("At last!").[21]

---

21. Some Christians are justifiably concerned about the dangers of alcohol and alcoholism, and while Scripture addresses these concerns (Gen. 9:21; Prov. 20:1; Eph. 5:18), it also speaks frequently about the blessings of wine and drink (Gen. 14:18; Deut. 14:26; Eccl. 10:19; Isa. 55:1; Joel 2:24; 1 Tim. 5:23).

Third, Jesus provides unexpectedly. From John's gospel, we are familiar with the portrayal of Jesus as the Word become Flesh (1:14), as the Good Shepherd (10:11), as the Way, the Truth, and the Life (14:6), but not as the Great Liquor Provider (2:9). Many images may come to mind when we think of Jesus, but they probably don't involve his bringing massive quantities of alcohol to a party. Jesus' wedding gift is not only abundant and excellent, but it's also unexpected. Just as Jesus' gift of wine for a wedding is surprising, God's gift of sex is surprising. Many Christians are shocked to discover that the first commandment is basically a command to have a lot of sex. We don't typically associate sex with God, but it's clear from Scripture that the divine gift for the first humans is a gift for all married couples. The divine gifts of Genesis 1 and John 2, sex and wine, are often linked in Scripture. While alcohol can be abused for sexual exploitation (in chapter 6 we'll discuss how Lot's daughters do this), it can also be used responsibly in contexts of celebration, love, and intimacy. The Song of Songs often connects love and wine: "your love is better than wine" (Song 1:2); "your mouth [is] like the best wine" (Song 7:9); "I would give you spiced wine to drink, the juice of my pomegranate" (Song 8:2). For those of you who are married, try reading that to your spouse and see what happens.

The story of John 2 has deep personal significance for Shannon and me. On June 23, 1991, when the two of us became one, the text for our wedding sermon was Jesus turning the water into wine. As we've tried to invite Jesus into our marriage and our family, we've consistently found him to be an abundant, excellent provider of unexpected good things. Before we invited Jesus into our marriage, we invited him into our engagement.

Inviting Jesus into Our Engagement

Shannon and I met as freshmen in college at an InterVarsity Christian Fellowship (IVCF) retreat, but it wasn't exactly love at first sight. (The "bone of my bones" declaration came thirty-one years later.) I am not permitted to publish my first memories of her from the retreat, but her first memory of me was from a skit of a simulated seeker Bible study. I played stoned-out druggie Hashish Jones. It is often said that my performance must have inspired Sean Penn as he played Jeff Spicoli two years later (1982) in that cinematic classic *Fast Times at Ridgemont High*. The consensus of the critics other than Shannon was that my portrayal was definitely Oscar worthy.

Over our college careers, we knew of each other as we were involved in IVCF groups in the San Francisco Bay Area, but we didn't become close friends. Eventually, we both joined the IVCF staff in the Los Angeles area, and we worked together at the Claremont Colleges. It took almost nine years to get from introduction to first date, but as we worked alongside each other in ministry, we fell in love ("At last!").

After dating for about six months, we wanted some input on whether we should move to a deeper level of commitment. So we invited our partners in campus ministry (Derek, Lisa, Tim, Julie, Alison, and Dan) to discuss our relationship with us. We talked and prayed. They asked tough questions about compatibility and potential problems with crossbreeding. (She's a fish, Shannon Trout; I'm a mammal, David Lamb.) After a couple of difficult hours, there was a positive consensus about the future of our relationship. About a week later, with the confidence of our community and with the blessing of our parents, we became engaged.

It was scary to trust our friends with the future of our relationship, but we knew that by including sisters and brothers in Christ, we were inviting not only the representatives of Jesus' body but also Jesus himself into our relationship. We have experienced the love of God, both Old Testament and New Testament styles, as he has provided abundantly, excellently, and unexpectedly over the course of our more than two decades together as husband and wife.

Unfortunately, however, many biblical marriages don't involve just one wife for one husband, as we'll see in the next chapter.

CHAPTER 3

POLYGAMISTS

Restroom Man + Restroom Woman

An infographic titled "Marriage according to the Bible"[1] has been circulating for a while on Facebook, Twitter, and blogs. It includes eight happy "couples." In each, Restroom Man is paired with various incarnations of Restroom Woman (the symbols for male and female found on all the world's restrooms; in case you've never visited a restroom, he's slightly taller, no dress). The infographic includes biblical references and examples. Here's a summary of the eight scenarios:

1. Man + Woman
2. Man + Brother's Widow (Levirate Marriage)
3. Man + Wives + Concubine
4. Rapist + His Victim (Restroom Woman's dress is ripped)
5. Man + Woman + Woman's Property
6. Male Soldier + Prisoner of War
7. Man + Woman + Woman + Woman ...
8. Male Slave + Female Slave

---

1. Here is a link for "Marriage according to the Bible": *http://imgur.com/yXkyl.*

The person posting the infographic typically adds a snarky comment about how outrageous it is to speak of a biblical "ideal" when the Bible upholds so many models for "marriage": polygamy, rape, concubines, prisoners of war, and so on.

My initial response is to chuckle and appreciate the clever nature of the infographic. Yours should be, "Hey, didn't I just read a chapter arguing for the biblical ideal for marriage?"

So does the Bible have an ideal for marriage or not?

If you read chapter 2, you know that I think it does, but I also think it is problematic enough to warrant writing a book about the non-ideal versions of marriage the Bible seems to condone.

While I will wait to go into the details of why this infographic is misleading, at this point I will simply say its designer confuses *is* with *ought*. For the biblical models of marriage that include numerous examples (for example, number 3, concubinage; and number 7, polygamy), the infographic fails to cite a relevant law that clearly supports the practice. For the models that cite a relevant law (for example, number 4, rapist; and number 6, prisoner of war), it lacks examples of the unorthodox practice. But we're getting ahead of ourselves; as we go through this chapter, we'll talk more about this distinction between descriptive and prescriptive texts. While the infographic is problematic on several levels, it is relevant to this chapter because it depicts not only a polygamous marriage (7) but also three other scenarios related to polygamy: levirate marriages (2), concubines (3), and prisoner wives (6).

Big Love and Sister Wives

Some of you may be wondering, "Why are we even talking about polygamy? Isn't that something they practice only in remote parts of the world (and Utah)?" Good question. I see three reasons why the topic of polygamy is relevant.

First, the issue is big on the small screen. In the past few years, US TV networks have been creating shows focusing on the topic. HBO's

Big Love (2006–2011) tells the ongoing fictional saga of the Mormon family of Bill and his three wives, Barb, Nicki, and Margie, who live in … Utah. TLC's *Sister Wives* (2010–ongoing) is a reality show centered on Cody and his four wives, Meri, Janelle, Christine, and Robyn, who live in … Utah (originally, but they moved to Las Vegas). The networks think polygamy is interesting enough for American audiences.

Second, we live in a global village (trite, but true). People in Africa watch American TV, and US magazines like *Christianity Today* discuss the topic of polygamy in Africa. Two separate recent *Christianity Today* articles discuss the tensions surrounding the issue of polygamy in the African church.[2] Many traditional Western missionaries to Africa called men in polygamous marriages to immediately cut back to one wife, divorcing extra wives. When the only African convert of Christian medical missionary David Livingstone was forced to choose, he left the faith and returned to polygamy. Because of their ignorance of the complexity of the African context, Christians developed the reputation as the group that promoted divorce.

Third, the Bible talks about polygamy a lot, including many examples of its practitioners (e.g., Abraham, Jacob, Moses, Gideon, David, and Solomon). Conscientious readers are going to ask about it since it makes no sense to those of us who live in contexts where it is illegal or viewed as backward. I've been asked by many friends and students, "What do we do with all these biblical polygamists?" We'll take a look at some of them soon, but first we need to examine the polygamy laws of the Old Testament.

Biblical Laws: Polygamy Happens

The Restroom Man infographic assumes that the abundance of polygamists in the Old Testament means that God's Word is

---

2. The two polygamy articles are Susan Wunderink, "What to Do about Unbiblical Unions," *Christianity Today*, June 25, 2009, *http://www.christianitytoday.com/ct/2009/july/12.17.html*; and Moses Wasamu, "The Polygamy Bill Dividing Kenya's Christians," *Christianity Today*, May 1, 2014, *http://www.christianitytoday.com/ct/2014/may/polygamy-bill-dividing-kenyas-christians.html*.

pro-polygamy. But just because the Bible includes a lot of polygamists doesn't mean that it endorses the practice.

Narrative texts can be difficult to interpret since readers are often uncertain whether a story is meant to be descriptive or prescriptive. Does the text simply describe what happened, which will include both good and bad behavior, or does it prescribe what should happen? It takes wisdom to decide.

Legal texts, however, are meant to be interpreted prescriptively. They are saying, "Here is what you should do." We need to ask if these laws, which are more than several thousand years old, still apply to the people of God today. But the relevant laws give us a good idea whether the Bible thinks polygamy is a good idea or a bad one.

As we saw in the previous chapter, Scripture clearly speaks of the monogamous ideal (e.g., Gen. 2:24). No Old Testament laws explicitly forbid polygamy, but neither do any explicitly encourage or affirm it.[3] It was simply assumed to be part of life. To utilize the vernacular, "polygamy happens."

For example, one law regarding inheritance among children of different wives begins, "If a man has two wives …" (Deut. 21:15). The law isn't affirming or condemning polygamy; it's merely addressing how to deal with some of the problems that might ensue from it. We know from Genesis and other texts that it's not ideal, but non-ideal scenarios occur all the time, so it's realistic to anticipate them and figure out how to legislate toward the ideal and to guarantee the rights of all members of the family.

Now let's look at the relevant laws.

---

3. See also the discussions of laws related to concubines and polygamy in David L. Baker, *Tight Fists or Open Hands? Wealth and Poverty in Old Testament Law* (Grand Rapids, Mich.: Eerdmans, 2009), 150–59; in Christopher J. H. Wright, *Old Testament Ethics for the People of God* (Downers Grove, Ill.: InterVarsity, 2004), 330–31; in Paul Copan, *Is God a Moral Monster?* (Grand Rapids, Mich.: Baker, 2011), 110–23.

Legislating Polygamy: Slaves and Sisters, Kings and Prisoners

The books of Exodus, Leviticus, and Deuteronomy contain five separate laws addressing polygamous family situations and involving five distinct types of wives (slave, sister, royal, prisoner, and levirate). Four of these scenarios (all except royal wives) are caricatured in the Restroom Man infographic.

The Slave Wife Law (or the No Family Plaything Law) attempts to insure the rights of concubines.

> When a man sells his daughter as a slave [or "**concubine**"[4]], she shall not go out as the male slaves do. If she does not please her master, who has designated her for himself, then he shall let her be redeemed. He shall have no right to sell her to a foreign people, since he has broken faith with her. If he designates her for his son, he shall deal with her as with a daughter. If he takes another **wife** to himself, he shall not diminish her food, her clothing, or her marital rights. And if he does not do these three things for her, she shall go out for nothing, without payment of money.
>
> — Exodus 21:7–11

The Old Testament speaks into a context where polygamy seems to be inevitable, so this law in particular attempts to improve the situation of the slave wife or concubine, since she is the weaker party. In case you've never met one, a concubine was simply a secondary wife, usually of lower social status, often a slave. Later in this chapter, we'll talk about Hagar, Abraham's concubine, and while the parallels are not perfect, the Slave Wife Law lists three beneficial rights for concubines like Hagar.

First, if things don't work out, she can't be resold as a slave. The man can keep her or allow her to be redeemed, presumably by her own

---

4. Baker translates *'amah* as "concubine," which makes more sense than "slave" in this context (*Tight Fists*, 152).

parents. Thus, she can't be traded for profit but gets to remain with her husband or her birth family. Second, she can't be a wife of both a father and a son, which Wright refers to as a "family plaything."[5] She is to be respected as the wife of one and only one member of the family. Third, she must be supported with food, clothes, and marital rights by the husband, even if he gets another wife. Thus, she is guaranteed to have social security. (I, however, have no guarantee of Social Security, since my generation is following the baby boomers.) David Baker makes an interesting point here about the concubine conjugal rights supported by this law: "Sex was not understood to be exclusively for the benefit of males in ancient Israel."[6] He was supposed to give her some food and "some lovin'."

The Sister Wife Law (or the What Was Laban Thinking Law) prohibits a man from having two sisters as wives.

> And you shall not take a woman as a rival **wife** to her sister, uncovering her nakedness while her sister is still alive.
> —Leviticus 18:18

This law theoretically prevented the type of dysfunctional family situation that Laban put his son-in-law Jacob in centuries earlier by giving him both of his daughters, Leah and Rachel, as wives (Gen. 29:21–28). While Copan believes this law forbids polygamy generally, Wenham's argument is more persuasive that the Hebrew here isn't referring to polygamy generally but is merely the marrying of multiple sisters by the same man.[7] The use of the expression "rival wife" (*tsarar,* a verb in Hebrew) suggests that this law was an attempt to reduce the type of family tension that characterized Jacob's family. This law protected women from contexts in which they would be competing with a sister for the affection of a husband.

The Royal Wife Law (or the What Was Solomon Thinking Law) sets a limit on spouses for kings.

---

5. Wright, *Old Testament Ethics,* 331.

6. Baker, *Tight Fists,* 159.

7. Copan, *Moral Monster,* 112–13; Gordon J. Wenham, *The Book of Leviticus* (Grand Rapids, Mich.: Eerdmans, 1979), 258.

> And he [the king] shall not acquire many **wives** for himself, lest his heart turn away, nor shall he acquire for himself excessive silver and gold.
>
> — Deuteronomy 17:17

The broader context of this law also limits, in addition to wives, a ruler's horses (v. 16) and gold. Typically, only wealthy men could afford to provide for multiple wives or concubines. Rulers, the 0.01 percent of their day, could have a harem with many wives. Thus, this law restricts the king, not for the sake of the women per se but for the sake of his spiritual condition, so he would not be led astray by the worship of foreign gods,[8] which presumably was bad also for his wives. The laws regarding slave and sister wives seem to look back to the time of Abraham and Jacob, and this law seems to look forward to the time of Solomon.[9] While Deuteronomy 17 is a bit vague about what "many wives" means, it's safe to say Solomon exceeded the limit well before he reached seven hundred wives and three hundred concubines (1 Kings 11:3).

The Prisoner-of-War Wife Law (or the Beautiful Bald Foreigner Law) provides protection for foreign wives.

> When you go out to war against your enemies, and the LORD your God gives them into your hand and you take them captive, and you see among the captives a beautiful woman, and you desire to take her to be your **wife**, and you bring her home to your house, she shall shave her head and pare her nails. And she shall take off the clothes in which she was captured and shall remain in your house and lament her father and her mother a full month. After that you may go in to her and be her husband, and she shall be your **wife**. But if you no longer delight in her, you shall let her go where she wants. But you shall not sell her for money, nor shall you treat her as a slave, since you have humiliated her.
>
> — Deuteronomy 21:10–14

8. Many royal marriages resulted from treaties with foreign nations (1 Kings 11:1; 16:31).
9. While many scholars believe the narratives and laws of the Pentateuch were written during the Israelite monarchy or later, here I won't discuss compositional dating issues but will simply engage the text in its canonical order.

Despite what the Restroom Man infographic suggests, the law regarding female captives is concerned primarily with protecting the foreign prisoner-of-war wife. While rape was tragically often a consequence of ancient military situations (see chapter 5), not only is it excluded here, but if a man desires a beautiful foreign woman, he can take her only as a wife, not as a slave.[10] If he isn't satisfied, she can be let go, but not as a slave; she can't be sold and, therefore, has the same rights as someone who is divorced. Additionally, this law is shockingly compassionate when compared with other ancient Near Eastern laws, because she is allowed to mourn for her loss for a month (bald head, pared nails) before the husband can "go in to her" (Deut. 21:13). Baker states, "Kindness toward concubines advocated in the biblical laws, especially Deuteronomy 21, is an advance over the matter-of-fact treatment of those in Mesopotamia."[11]

The Levirate Wife Law (or the Marry Your Brother-in-Law Law) sets up a system to give security to childless widows.

> If brothers dwell together, and one of them dies and has no son, the **wife** of the dead man shall not be married outside the family to a stranger. Her husband's brother shall go in to her and take her as his **wife** and perform the duty of a husband's brother to her. And the first son whom she bears shall succeed to the name of his dead brother, that his name may not be blotted out of Israel.
>
> — Deuteronomy 25:5–6

The expression "levirate marriage" comes from the Latin, *levir*, for "brother-in-law." The Levirate Wife Law doesn't sound as creepy as the Marry Your Brother-in-Law Law, but they mean the same thing. The law says that when a man dies without an heir, his brother has sex with his wife to perpetuate his brother's line. The law has

---

10. While the phrase "you have humiliated her" (from the verb *'anah*) could seem violent, in this context it merely suggests that they have had sex; see Baker, *Tight Fists*, 155n80. The related noun (*'onah*) is used to refer to a concubine's right to sex with her husband (Exod. 21:10).

11. Baker, *Tight Fists*, 159.

two concerns: first to provide an heir to the dead man, and second to provide for the needs of the childless widow. This law may seem unfamiliar, foreign, and probably just plain weird today, but that was not the case in ancient Israel, where it was meant to help widows in a vulnerable situation. I'll discuss Tamar in the next chapter, but her actions support the conclusion that levirate marriage was designed to benefit the widow. And if her brother-in-law refused to have sex with her, she got to humiliate him in front of the elders by stealing his sandal, insulting him, and spitting in his face (Deut. 25:9–10). A video of that would go viral on YouTube. Once again, the law is given to guarantee the rights of the weaker party, in this case the deceased man and his widow.

In these polygamous family situations, these laws are designed to bless the entire family by reducing tension (Sister Law), by encouraging spiritual welfare (Royal Law), by providing security (Slave Law, Levirate Law), and by insuring respect and honor for all parties (Slave Law, Levirate Law, Prisoner Law). The laws may not make sense to us (and obviously not to the designer of the infographic), since we don't have concubines, extra spouses, or prisoners of war living with us. (At least I don't; you might.) But in the world of ancient Israel, where all of those situations were common, they made sense because they guaranteed a radical humanizing protection for marginalized women.

While it may be obvious to any of you familiar with these legal texts, it is still worth stating: the context makes it clear that these laws were given to Moses from Yahweh. God inspired them. God set up the ideal for marriage in Genesis, but in a non-ideal world, he gave laws to protect the rights of everyone involved: wives, husbands, sisters, kings, slaves, widows, concubines, and prisoners. Even though love, Old Testament style, was not always ideal, God still loved polygamists and their families.

A Plethora of Polygamists

Later in this chapter, we'll examine three polygamists in depth, but first I want to give you a glimpse of how many polygamists there were in the Old Testament. I've constructed a table of twenty-nine biblical polygamists, with the husband's name, the number of his wives (W) and concubines (C), their names (if known), and relevant biblical references.

Biblical Polygamists			
Husband	**Number**	**Wives and Concubines** (if names are known)	**References**
Lamech	2 W	Adah, Zillah	Gen. 4:19–24
Abraham	2 W + 1 C	Sarah, Hagar (C), Keturah	Gen. 11:29; 16:3; 25:1, 6
Nahor	1 W + 1 C	Milcah, Reumah (C)	Gen. 22:23–24
Esau	3 W	Judith, Basemath, Mahalath	Gen. 26:34; 28:9
Jacob	2 W + 2 C	Leah, Rachel, Bilhah (C), Zilpah (C)	Gen. 29:23, 28; 30:4, 9; 35:22
Eliphaz	1 W + 1 C	Timna (C)	Gen. 36:12
Moses	2 W	Zipporah, a Cushite[a]	Exod. 2:21; Num. 12:1
Gideon	Many W + 1 C		Judg. 8:30–31
Elkanah	2 W	Hannah, Peninnah	1 Sam. 1:2
Saul	1 W + 1 C	Ahinoam, Rizpah (C)	1 Sam. 14:50; 2 Sam. 3:7; 12:8
David	Many W + 10 C	Michal, Abigail, Ahinoam, Haggith, Abital, Eglah, Bathsheba, Maacah (+ 10 C)	1 Sam. 18:27; 25:42–43; 2 Sam. 3:3–5; 5:13; 12:7–8, 24; 15:16
Absalom	10 C	He went into 10 of David's C's	2 Sam. 16:22
Solomon	1000	= 700 W (Naamah) + 300 C	1 Kings 11:3; 14:21
Ahab	W's	Jezebel	1 Kings 20:3, 7
Jerahmeel	2 W	Atarah	1 Chron. 2:26
Caleb	2 C		1 Chron. 2:46, 48

Biblical Polygamists (continued)			
Husband	**Number**	**Wives and Concubines** (if names are known)	**References**
Ashhur	2 W	Helah, Naarah	1 Chron. 4:5
Mered	4 W	Jehudijah, Bithiah, Hodiah	1 Chron. 4:17–19
Manasseh	1 W + 1 C		1 Chron. 7:14
Machir	2 W	Maacah, Zelophehad	1 Chron. 7:15–16
Shaharaim	2 W	Hushim, Baara	1 Chron. 8:8
Rehoboam	18 W + 60 C	Mahalath, Maacah	2 Chron. 11:18–21; 13:2
Abijah	14 W	Maacah?	2 Chron. 13:21; 1 Kings 15:10
Jehoram	W's	Athaliah	2 Chron. 21:6; 22:2
Joash	2 W	Jehoaddan	2 Chron. 24:3; 25:1
Jehoiachin	W's		2 Kings 24:15
Zedekiah	W's		Jer. 38:23
Belshazzar	W's		Dan. 5:2
Ahasuerus	> 2 W	Vashti, Esther	Est. 1:9; 2:14, 17

ª Some scholars think Moses' "Cushite" wife refers to Zipporah, but she is usually described as Midianite (Exod. 2:15–21; 18:1–2). See Gordon J. Wenham, *Numbers: An Introduction and Commentary* (Downers Grove, Ill.: InterVarsity, 1981), 110–11.

There are at least twenty-nine polygamists in the Old Testament.[12] A plethora of polygamists. Despite this high number, scholars think that the vast majority of marriages in Israel were monogamous, since a man had to be wealthy to support multiple wives.[13] Many of these twenty-nine polygamists were rulers (thirteen total), and others were important leaders, tribal leaders, and patriarchs. In ancient Israel it would have been unusual for a common man to have multiple wives.

12. It is likely that other men in the Old Testament were polygamists, but this table includes only the ones where the text makes their polygamy explicit.
13. See Baker, *Tight Fists*, 157; Wright, *Old Testament Ethics*, 330.

August 19 Is Polygamy Day

The website *BiblicalPolygamy.com* argues that since there are so many biblical polygamists, the Bible supports polygamy. (While perusing the site, I also discovered that August 19 is Polygamy Day; be sure to mark your calendar.) The fact that the Bible includes a lot of polygamists doesn't mean that it condones the practice or that God supports it. The Bible includes far more idol worshipers, and yet the practice is still severely condemned.

Looking at what types of people were polygamists will help us determine whether the Old Testament affirms or condemns the practice. We won't be able to discuss all twenty-nine of these polygamists in depth, so hopefully you'll pardon my lumping them into three categories: the Good, the Bad, and the Unclear. (The text doesn't typically comment on appearance, but some may have also been ugly.)[14]

The Good are the men who are portrayed positively in the text. There are seven Good (= 24 percent of these twenty-nine polygamists): two patriarchs (Abraham and Jacob), one lawgiver (Moses), one judge (Gideon), one father of a prophet (Elkanah, father of Samuel), and two righteous kings (David and Joash). The Bad are men who are portrayed negatively in the text, most of whom are rulers who receive a royal condemnation: "They did evil in the eyes of Yahweh." There are thirteen Bad (= 45 percent; Lamech, Esau, Saul, Absalom, Solomon, Ahab, Rehoboam, Abijah, Jehoram, Jehoiachin, Zedekiah, Belshazzar, and Ahasuerus). The Unclear are men we don't know enough about to make a clear evaluation. There are nine Unclear (= 31 percent; Nahor, Eliphaz, Jerahmeel, Caleb, Ashhur, Mered, Manasseh, Machir, Shaharaim).

While we might hope for a clear pattern of bad polygamists and good monogamists, the biblical data does not provide overwhelming support for such a pattern. The Bads make up the largest group by far, but three of the Good ones are men who are widely perceived to be heroes of the faith (Abraham, Moses, and David). The fact that far more polygamists are portrayed negatively than positively undermines

---

14. I realize these categorizations are rather subjective.

the argument of *BiblicalPolygamy.com*, but to determine more clearly the biblical perspective on this issue, we need to examine some of these polygamists in more depth.

Lamech, His Ornament, and His Shadow

As we look for evidence that polygamy might not have been a good thing, we need to look no farther than the next two wives mentioned by name in the Bible after Eve: Adah and Zillah. Their husband, Lamech, the first polygamist, was a bad guy.

> And Lamech took two **wives**. The name of the one was Adah [Ornament], and the name of the other Zillah [Shadow]. Adah bore Jabal; he was the father of those who dwell in tents and have livestock. His brother's name was Jubal; he was the father of all those who play the lyre and pipe. Zillah also bore Tubal-cain; he was the forger of all instruments of bronze and iron. The sister of Tubal-cain was Naamah.
>
> Lamech said to his wives:
>
> > "Adah and Zillah, hear my voice;
> >   you **wives** of Lamech, listen to what I say:
> > I have killed a man for wounding me,
> >   a young man for striking me.
> > If Cain's revenge is sevenfold,
> >   then Lamech's is seventy-sevenfold."
> >   — Genesis 4:19–24

Notice first the names of his wives. Adah means "ornament" (Isa. 49:18; Ezek. 16:11) and Zillah means "shadow" (Ps. 144:4; 2 Kings 20:9). They sound like trophy wives, his Ornament and his Shadow. Not exactly the helper-partner, the *'ezer kenegdo*, we saw in Genesis 2. Polygamy gets off to a bad start, at least in terms of empowerment for women.

Lamech's only recorded words to his wives are a stark contrast to Adam's first words to Eve: "Adah, Zillah, hear my voice ..." Eve was greeted with a love poem (Gen. 2:23), Adah and Zillah with a taunt poem. I'm not the most romantic guy, but even I think most women would prefer Adam's poem over Lamech's. Lamech sounds like a cave man.

What does Lamech tell his wives? He brags about killing someone for merely wounding him. Most English translations have "young man" as the second victim, but the Hebrew word *yeled* usually means someone younger and is often translated elsewhere as "child" or "boy." The NASB has "boy" for *yeled* here, which makes more sense than "young man" in this context. One can see a logical three-step progression from killing a man, then killing a boy, then potentially killing a woman. From the first two lines of his speech, he clearly wants his wives to hear his thinly veiled threat.

If Lamech was trying to impress his wives, we could call it a misguided attempt at being macho. But it's more likely that he was threatening them, essentially verbal abuse, which would mean he's potentially an abuser of women as well as children (the boy he killed). I can think of a lot of words to describe Lamech, but most of them would not be approved by my editors.

Lamech established a precedent not only for bigamy and abuse but also for the military escalation principle (you wound me, I kill you). The text doesn't explicitly condemn polygamy here, but it makes the polygamist look evil. Let's see what happens with the next polygamist; you may have heard of him.

Father Abraham Had Many Wives

Depending on which version of the children's song you prefer, Father Abraham, after a long wait, had either "many" or "seven" sons. But I'm pretty sure they did other things than "go like this." If you count Ishmael, Abraham actually had eight sons.[15] In addition to divine intervention (in the case of Sarah), what helped him have

---

15. Sarah and Hagar each had one son (Isaac and Ishmael), but Keturah had six (Zimran, Jokshan, Medan, Midian, Ishbak and Shuah; see Gen. 25:2).

so many sons was the fact that he had three wives: Sarah, Hagar, and Keturah. Perhaps we should change the song?

> Father Abraham had many wives,
> Many wives had Father Abraham.

According to the order of Genesis, it might appear that Abraham didn't take Keturah as a wife until Sarah was dead (Gen. 23:1–2; 25:1), but two factors suggest that Abraham married Keturah while Sarah was alive. First, the text calls Keturah a "concubine" (Gen. 25:6; 1 Chron. 1:32), which usually implies that there was another primary wife. Second, some might think it difficult (pre-Viagra) for a man in his fourteenth, fifteenth, or sixteenth decade (he was 137 when Sarah died) to be fathering sons. Most scholars think the union happened much earlier.[16]

While it's impossible to be certain, I think these two wives overlapped. In any case, Abraham was already a polygamist, since the text calls Hagar his wife while he was married to Sarah. Let's look at that story.[17]

> And Sarai said to Abram, "Behold now, the **LORD** has prevented me from bearing children. Go in to my servant; it may be that I shall obtain children by her." And Abram listened to the voice of Sarai. So, after Abram had lived ten years in the land of Canaan, Sarai, Abram's wife, took Hagar the Egyptian, her servant, and gave her to Abram her husband as a wife. And he went in to Hagar, and she conceived. And when she saw that she had conceived, she looked with contempt on her mistress. And Sarai said to Abram, "May the wrong done to me be on you! I gave my servant to your

---

16. For example, see Derek Kidner, *Genesis* (Downers Grove, Ill.: InterVarsity, 1967), 150; Gordon J. Wenham, *Genesis 1–15* (Waco, Tex.: Word, 1987), 158.

17. For an in-depth academic discussion of Hagar, see Phyllis Trible, *Texts of Terror: Literary-Feminist Readings of Biblical Narratives* (Philadelphia: Fortress, 1984), 8–35. For an insightful spiritual discussion of the narratives of Sarah and Hagar, see Carolyn Custis James, *Lost Women of the Bible* (Grand Rapids, Mich.: Zondervan, 2005), 65–100.

embrace, and when she saw that she had conceived, she looked on me with contempt. May the **Lord** judge between you and me!" But Abram said to Sarai, "Behold, your servant is in your power; do to her as you please." Then Sarai dealt harshly with her, and she fled from her.

—Genesis 16:2–6

This text calls both Sarah and Hagar the wife of Abraham. Notice that the polygamous union was Sarah's idea, not Abraham's.[18] It wasn't for Abraham's sexual pleasure (although he didn't complain); it was for producing children. While God didn't explicitly condemn this union, neither did he authorize it. And God later makes it clear that only the child through Sarah was to be the son of the promise (Gen. 17:18–21; 22:2). The text is clear here: polygamy is not the ideal.

We see the non-ideal nature of this polygamous union in its outcomes, as tension and oppression result from it. Hagar conceives right away (one pitch, one hit), so she looks at Sarah with contempt, which prompts Sarah to rebuke her husband. Abraham attempts to defuse the tension by reminding her that Hagar is still under her authority. It's hard to know exactly what it entailed, but Sarah's harsh treatment was sufficiently abusive for a newly pregnant mother to decide it was safer to flee into an arid wilderness than to remain under an oppressive mistress, even with food, water, and housing.

Unlike the marital abuse of Lamech, the first polygamist, here the abuse comes primarily from the other wife, Sarah. However, the patriarch Abraham doesn't step in to advocate for Hagar, despite the fact that she's carrying his child. Hagar was already vulnerable as a foreign slave living among Abraham's family, but now she's an expectant mother in the desert with no one to help her.

---

18. Hagar's silence begs the question, was Hagar raped by Abraham? I certainly hope she wasn't. As a servant, she probably viewed the shift from slave to concubine as a promotion; that's how it was viewed in her society. In the two chapters after the Hagar chapter, Trible (*Texts of Terror*) discusses rape victims, so presumably she would have noted it if she had perceived that Hagar was raped.

God Sees Hagar

But God is looking out for Hagar.

> The angel of the **LORD** **found** her by a spring of water in the wilderness, the spring on the way to Shur. And he said, "Hagar, servant of Sarai, **where** have you come from and **where** are you going?" She said, "I am fleeing from my mistress Sarai." The angel of the **LORD** said to her, "Return to your mistress and submit to her." The angel of the **LORD** also said to her, "I will surely multiply your offspring so that they cannot be numbered for multitude." And the angel of the **LORD** said to her,
>
> > "Behold, you are pregnant
> > > and shall bear a son.
> > You shall call his name Ishmael,
> > > because the **LORD** has listened to your affliction.
> > He shall be a wild donkey of a man,
> > > his hand against everyone
> > > and everyone's hand against him,
> > and he shall dwell over against all his kinsmen."
>
> So she called the name of the **LORD** who spoke to her, "You are a **God** of seeing," for she said, "Truly here I have seen him who looks after me."
>
> — Genesis 16:7–13

While the interaction between Hagar and the angel of Yahweh isn't entirely positive for Hagar ("go back and submit," and the "wild donkey" prophecy), she still receives it positively since she concludes that God is looking after her. The text also records that God seeks her, finds her, and listens to her affliction. When Hagar was alone, oppressed, and vulnerable, God was taking care of her.

After Hagar returns, Ishmael is born, and eventually Sarah gives birth to Isaac, but she doesn't like how Ishmael and young Isaac play together, so Hagar is driven into the wilderness a second time, where

God again appears to the Egyptian servant, providing for her and her son and promising that he'll become a great nation (Gen. 21:8–21), which in that culture in particular was a great honor for any mother. In both of her oppression scenarios, while Abraham and Sarah argue about what to do with Hagar, they ignore her and she is silent. But Yahweh doesn't ignore her; he sees her, engages her, asks her questions, listens to her, and provides for her.[19]

From the story of Abraham the polygamist we can make two points. First, just as we saw with Lamech, since it resulted in a pattern of spousal abuse, polygamy was not ideal. Second, just as he did with the polygamy laws, God worked to provide for the abused in a non-ideal polygamous context.

Jacob the Reluctant Polygamist

Jacob, the grandson of Abraham, didn't want more than one wife. He wanted Rachel, just her. But after Jacob worked for seven years for her, Rachel's father, Laban, manages to give him Rachel's sister, Leah, on his wedding night, and somehow he doesn't notice until the next day.

> Then Jacob said to Laban, "Give me my **wife** that I may go in to her, for my time is completed." So Laban gathered together all the people of the place and made a feast. But in the evening he took his daughter Leah and brought her to Jacob, and he went in to her. (Laban gave his female servant Zilpah to his daughter Leah to be her servant.) And in the morning, behold, it was Leah! And Jacob said to Laban, "What is this you have done to me? Did I not serve with you for Rachel? Why then have you deceived me?"
>
> — Genesis 29:21–25

---

19. Yahweh legislates a comparable situation when he declares that the son of a less-favored wife (Ishmael, son of Hagar) should not lose the firstborn's double-inheritance to a younger son of a more favored wife (Isaac, son of Sarah; Deut. 21:15–17).

It's hard to know exactly how the sister switcheroo could have happened. I assume it was a combination of wine, veils, and bad lighting. While Leah was the first wife, Rachel was the loved wife. But apparently Jacob loved Leah enough to sleep with her at least seven times, and she cranks out six sons and a daughter (Reuben, Simeon, Levi, Judah, Issachar, Zebulun, and Dinah), while Rachel remains barren. Even though the surrogate mother thing didn't work out great with her husband's grandparents, Rachel thinks she'll give it another chance, so she offers her maid Bilhah to Jacob as a concubine and, lo and behold, two more sons appear (Dan and Naphtali). Leah, not to be outdone, then offers Jacob her concubine, Zilpah, who proves equally fertile (Gad and Asher). Eventually Rachel has two boys (Joseph and Benjamin), tragically dying during childbirth for the latter.

Notice that each of the extra wives were the idea of someone other than Jacob (Laban, Rachel, and Leah). Jacob was a reluctant polygamist. Like his grandfather, he didn't offer any resistance, but there isn't a hint that these unions were to fulfill his sexual desires. In each case the reason for another wife was to produce more children. And produce they did. Jacob's four wives gave birth to twelve sons (Gen. 29:31–30:24; 35:16–18), and their descendants became the twelve tribes of Israel, which, interestingly, was the name God had given to Jacob after an all-night mud-wrestling match (Gen. 32:22–30). Abraham's family started slowly, but because of Jacob's polygamous family, many more "stars" were born.

We know from the first commission that God wanted his people to be fruitful and to multiply (Gen. 1:28). And in the spirit of this commission, God was working through Jacob's polygamous family to continue to fulfill the promise to Abraham to make him into a great nation (Gen. 12:2).

But polygamy is never ideal, and there wasn't competition only among these rival sister wives (as the Sister Wife Law later addressed); there was also serious animosity between their sons, culminating in the selling and enslavement of Joseph by his brothers (Gen. 37:26–28).

Yet God was still sovereign even in polygamous family situations, and while polygamy was not his choice for his people, he still chose to call his people Israel, the divinely given name of Jacob, the reluctant polygamist.

Polygamy Pros and Cons

By discussing the relevant laws, by looking briefly at all of the biblical polygamists, and in more depth at three of them (Lamech, Abraham, and Jacob), we see clear patterns regarding the pros and cons of Old Testament polygamy.

In terms of the consequences, polygamy leads to problems in families. Rival wives can become competitive and even oppressive. To the conflicts we've discussed between Sarah and Hagar, and Leah and Rachel, we can add the conflict between Peninnah and Hannah. (The latter was the mother of the prophet Samuel; 1 Sam. 1:2–6.) Sons from the same father but different mothers can have violent sibling rivalries. To the conflict between Jacob's sons, we can add the conflict between the sons of Gideon, as Abimelech killed his seventy brothers (Judg. 8:30–9:5); and the ones between the sons of David, as Absalom killed Amnon and Solomon killed Adonijah (2 Sam. 13:28–29; 1 Kings 2:24–25). Deuteronomy 17:17 predicted that foreign wives can lead rulers into idolatry, and this prediction proved accurate in the reigns of Solomon and Ahab (1 Kings 11:1–10; 16:31–33).

And yet God still works through this non-ideal form of marriage to bring about positive fruit, primarily children and security. When love, Old Testament style, was polygamous, God still loved the polygamous family. In the families of Abraham and Jacob, the driving factor toward having multiple wives was the desire to produce children, usually initiated by existing wives. The goal was primarily to provide sons, particularly within childless families. Providing security for wives, concubines, and children was one of the major concerns of the polygamy laws (especially the Slave, Levirate, and Prisoner laws). If the Slave Wife Law of Exodus 21 had already been instituted in the time of

Genesis 16, Hagar would have had more legal rights, and her abusive situation could have been prevented.

When I tell people I'm writing about polygamy, several friends have asked, "Was Boaz, the husband of Ruth, a polygamist?" We don't know about Boaz's marital status, since the text doesn't say, but as a respectable, wealthy, older man in Israelite society, it is likely that he already had a wife when he married Ruth, the Moabite widow. While the parallels are not perfect (Boaz is not the brother of Ruth's deceased husband), Boaz seems to be acting in the manner of levirate marriage here, willing to provide an heir for her first husband and a home for Ruth. Assuming Boaz was already married, his marriage to Ruth would be a good example of how, in a non-ideal world with a lot of widows like Ruth, polygamy was a good thing since it provided security for Ruth and her mother-in-law, Naomi. And through their union, God provided heirs, which included David and Jesus.

Should We Legalize Polygamy?

Most of us in the West are appalled by the practice of polygamy, which seems to us uncivilized. But Western Christians need to learn about this topic from people who live in contexts where polygamy is more acceptable, since their world is more comparable to the world of the Old Testament. I found an article on polygamy by an African Christian, David Gitari (who became the Anglican Archbishop of Kenya in 1997), to be particularly enlightening.[20] He concludes, as many of us probably would, that monogamy is God's ideal for marriage. But he also argues that the Christian church needs to be wiser and more sensitive in polygamous contexts. He also directly challenges Western attitudes toward polygamy and divorce.

> The African custom of having a second wife without discarding the first one is, in the opinion of the present writer, a *lesser* evil than the European custom of divorce and remarriage. In this respect, polygamy may be more "Christian" than divorce.

---

20. David Gitari, "The Church and Polygamy," *Transformation* 1 (1984), 3–10.

> A polygamist who respects tradition is normally expected to care for his wives and children, to give them security and indeed to love them. The divorced husband, on the other hand, completely severs his relationship with his wife and shows no more concern for her.[21]

Both Gitari and the polygamy laws of the Old Testament share a primary concern for the security of wives and children. Yes, polygamy seems wrong, but if it means that vulnerable women and children are provided for, then this non-ideal situation is preferable to the alternative. Gitari makes a valid point about how divorce in Europe (I would say the West) is normally viewed as less problematic than polygamy. Gitari also points out that polygamy makes sense when there are far more women than men in a society, which often happens in contexts of extended warfare, and it makes sense where culturally and economically women have fewer opportunities for independence. Gitari opened my eyes to my cultural arrogance, and his perspective allows me to better understand the world of sexuality and marriage in ancient Israel.

I also read an article in *Slate* written by a feminist, Jillian Keenan, who argues that the United States should "Legalize Polygamy," since she thinks it would provide more protection for women, children, and families.[22] While I don't agree with everything Keenan says, she makes a compelling argument for legalization. Don't worry, I still think polygamy isn't what God intended and shouldn't be legalized, but I will practice caution before condemning polygamous behavior in Scripture or in non-Western contexts. While Jesus didn't address the topic of polygamy directly, he did get asked about it, so let's turn there next.

---

21. Ibid., 8.
22. Jillian Keenan, "Legalize Polygamy! No. I Am Not Kidding," *Slate* (April 15, 2013), *http://www.slate.com/articles/double_x/doublex/2013/04/legalize_polygamy_marriage _equality_for_all.html.*

Jesus and the Polygamist at the Well

Polygamy isn't a big issue in the Gospels. When Jesus gets asked by the Sadducees[23] about a ridiculous, yet heavenly, scenario of one bride for seven brothers (Mark 12:18–27), he makes no comment about levirate marriage or polygamy and merely states that in the afterlife people won't be married but will be like angels (so harps and halos, presumably).

But the issue of multiple marriages comes up in the familiar story in John 4 of Jesus' interaction with the Samaritan woman at the well.[24] Jesus has been traveling with his disciples, and they make a stop at Jacob's well in Samaria. The disciples go into town to buy food, so Jesus is left at the well, and a Samaritan woman arrives to draw water.

While much has been said about how she must have been an outcast or even a prostitute, since she was avoiding people by coming to the well at noon (the sixth hour), the hottest time of the day, we shouldn't speculate about the woman's character based merely on when she visited the well this particular day. Yes, in biblical times most people normally collected water in the evening (Gen. 24:11), but I normally don't go to the grocery store at 5:00 because it's crowded, and yet there are still those rare instances when I need to shop then. That doesn't mean I'm a prostitute. Jesus came to the well at noon, but we don't think he's a prostitute.

Let's base our opinion of this woman on what the text states about her. As I tell my students, "When it comes to the Bible, don't make stuff up." There's a corollary: "Don't repeat stuff other people make up." So to be precise, the hottest time of the day isn't noon but later, usually between two and four. Also, we don't know how hot it was on the day Jesus interacted with this Samaritan woman. As I write this, I have just returned from my first trip to Israel, which was in the early spring (so not the heat of summer, but not the cold of winter either), and there

23. The Sadducees didn't believe in the afterlife, so they were *sad, you see.* I'm embarrassed about this pun, so I buried it in the footnotes.

24. For a discussion of the cultural background of this story, see Kenneth E. Bailey, *Jesus through Middle Eastern Eyes* (Downers Grove, Ill.: InterVarsity, 2008), 200–16.

were times when I was cold at noon. The text doesn't even say Jesus was thirsty, merely that he asks for a drink. Perhaps he's trying to start a conversation, the ancient equivalent of, "Can you buy me a drink?"

So Jesus asks her for a drink, which puts her in the power position as the one he is dependent upon. She's shocked because Jews don't normally talk to Samaritans, and, except for their wives, men don't normally talk to women. (Upon their return, the disciples are shocked more about the cross-gender than the cross-racial interaction; John 4:27.) Jesus quickly takes the conversation to a deeper, spiritual level when he speaks about living water, which piques her attention.

> The <u>woman</u> said to him, "Sir, give me this water, so that I will not be thirsty or have to come here to draw water."
> Jesus said to her, "Go, call your **husband**, and come here." The <u>woman</u> answered him, "I have no **husband**." Jesus said to her, "You are right in saying, 'I have no **husband**'; for you have had **five husbands**, and the one you now have is not your **husband**. What you have said is true." The <u>woman</u> said to him, "Sir, I perceive that you are a prophet."
>
> —John 4:15–19

Before giving her some of his living water, Jesus suggests that she get her husband, which prompts her to inform him about her lack of said husband. After affirming her for her honest response, Jesus explains that yes, technically, she doesn't have a husband, but she has in fact had five, and the man she's living with now isn't a proper husband. Sounds like the Sadducees' hypothetical scenario, one bride for six "husbands."

Notice that she doesn't correct Jesus but, with a sense of humor, shifts the focus back to Jesus: "Sir, I perceive that you're a prophet."

Five or six husbands—is she an adulterer, a prostitute, or just a loose woman? Before we leap into speculation land, let's look at what the text says about her marital history. The text includes nothing to suggest that she's a prostitute. There are no reasons given in the text why any of her five marriages ended, but we know that there are only two possible options: divorce or death.

She may have been *divorced* five times, which would be unusual, but not illegal. According to Old Testament law, it was not the wife but the husband who initiated divorce (Deut. 24:1; see also Deut. 22:19, 29). She may have done something to warrant divorce, but again, that's speculation. If divorce was in her past, we know that she wasn't the party instigating the separation.

She may have been *widowed* five times, which sounds a bit like Tamar (whom we'll discuss in chapter 4) or like Harriet in *So I Married an Axe Murderer.*[25] Wives were often younger than husbands, so biblically we see more widows than widowers. But unless this Samaritan woman killed her husbands, which doesn't seem likely, she can't be blamed for their deaths. Biblically, God's people are meant to show mercy toward widows (e.g., Exod. 22:22).

She is living with someone who's not her husband, which is a problem, but not enough of a problem for Jesus to condemn her for it. Most likely, it was a combination of divorce and death that ended her five marriages. Instead of viewing her with condemnation as a loose woman, we should view her with compassion as a victimized woman with a tragic life.

Unfortunately, we never learn her name, so she gets called the Woman at the Well or the Samaritan Woman. But neither of those characteristics is particularly distinguishing. Most women visit wells, and half of the Samaritans were female. (Just guessing here.) What is most unusual about this woman is that she's had five husbands, referred to today as a serial polygamist (assuming they didn't overlap).[26] I call her the Polygamist at the Well. We'll see if that catches on.

Throughout the Gospels, Jesus is curiously cryptic about his identity in his interactions with his disciples and religious leaders, but when this polygamous Samaritan woman brings up the topic of the Christ, Jesus clearly states, "I who speak to you am he" (John 4:26).

---

25. *So I Married an Axe Murderer* (1993) stars Nancy Travis as Harriet and Mike Myers as Charlie.

26. The *Psychology Dictionary* defines "serial polygamy" as "a person who repeatedly gets married and divorced many times in a lifetime" (*http://psychologydictionary.org/serial-polygamy/*).

In John's gospel, Jesus breaks down obstacles of gender and ethnicity to first reveal the secret of his identity to a polygamist.

Why did Jesus reveal himself to her? Because he loves polygamists. God uses messed up people to accomplish his purposes — polygamists like Abraham, Jacob, Moses, Gideon, David, and Solomon, and even the unnamed Samaritan polygamist at the well. She is also one of the first evangelists; she didn't allow her scandalous polygamous past to prevent her from speaking to the entire town about the man who "told me all that I ever did." If God can work through polygamists, he can work through you and me.

Why Did You Skip Polygamy?

One of the unique blessings of writing a book about the Bible is that people you have never met assume you can shed light on their most difficult biblical questions. A few months after *God Behaving Badly* came out, I received a gracious email from Sarah, who clearly appreciated the book but would have appreciated it more if I had mentioned one other subject.

> I do, however, wish that in the chapter on sexism you would have addressed the role of polygamy, especially where God tells David through the prophet that he would have gladly given him even more wives in confronting David about taking Bathsheba. I can't help but feel as though women were prized as virgins, but men could sleep around, and of course, I cannot imagine having a husband on Mondays, Wednesdays, and Fridays, while my sister or another woman had him on Tuesdays and Thursdays! If it were not for the David passage, I could dismiss it as God's people acting pagan, but that does not seem to be the take of Nathan. Any advice?

I was tempted to tell Sarah that polygamy does not involve God behaving badly but involves humans behaving badly; however, the framing of her question anticipated this objection as she focused on

God's apparent promise to provide even more wives for David (2 Sam. 12:8), which seems to constitute a divine endorsement of the practice.

Shortly after receiving Sarah's question, I was speaking to a group of church leaders about *God Behaving Badly*, so I asked them what they would say to Sarah. I included their insights in my response to Sarah.

First, about polygamy in general, one guy noted that it was considered the duty of a man who was well-off to have multiple wives in order to provide for more people, almost like Social Security. It's not just that women were objects or possessions but that a man who could afford to care for more people should do so as a social obligation.

Also, in 2 Samuel 12:8, the phrase "and if that had been too little, I would have added as much more" (NRSV) does not need to be limited to more wives. It's a reasonable assumption given the context, but in addition to wives, God has just told David that (1) he anointed him, (2) he rescued him from Saul, (3) he gave him the house of Israel and Judah. While it seems like more wives are implied, it's possible that God is just saying he would have been willing to give him other things, perhaps like what he does to Solomon in 1 Kings 3 — wisdom, riches, long life, etc.

And finally, God was accommodating himself to what happened with kings back then. God had set up the ideal in Genesis 2 — one man, one woman in a lifelong committed relationship. But he was willing to allow them to follow non-ideal patterns of their day. A bit like he did with the monarchy and the temple. Neither was his idea, and later he destroyed the temple and cut off the monarchy. It's pretty clear from the story of Solomon and Deuteronomy 17:17 that many wives is a bad thing, even for kings.

So, not exactly definitive solutions, but a few more pieces of the puzzle to move the conversation forward.

May God bless you as you keep working on these difficult issues in Scripture.

I'm still not fully satisfied with these answers to Sarah's question, but the three points in my email seem to effectively summarize the major themes from this discussion. I'd like to think of this chapter on biblical polygamy not only as a response to the Restroom Man infographic but also as a second draft of a response to my friend Sarah.

May God bless *you* as you keep working on these difficult issues in Scripture.

CHAPTER 4

PROSTITUTES

Prostitute Barbie?

We may be familiar with Mermaid Barbie, Explorer Barbie, or Lawyer Barbie, but what about Prostitute Barbie? It might not sound right, but it's truer than you'd expect. The creator of Barbie, Jack Ryan — not the Tom Clancy hero but the designer who worked for Mattel, the toy company — based Barbie's design on a German doll named Lilli, who was a character in a comic, basically a prostitute.[1] When told by a police officer that the two-piece swimming suit she was wearing was banned, Lilli replies, "Which piece do you want me to take off?"[2] Barbie's prototype was popularly known in Germany as a sex toy. Unlike Matthew in his genealogy of Jesus, Mattel doesn't normally highlight the scandalous ancestry of Barbie.

In an episode from the US television show *The West Wing*, Amy Gardner (Mary-Louise Parker) tells Josh Lyman (Bradley Whitford) that no little girls ever say, "I wanna be a prostitute when I grow up."[3]

1. John Walsh, "Barbie Was Based on a Cartoon Prostitute Who'd Do Anything for Money," *The Independent*, January 13, 2009, *http://www.independent.co.uk/voices/columnists/john-walsh-barbie-was-based-on-a-cartoon-prostitute-whod-do-anything-for-money-1331669.html*.
2.*http://en.wikipedia.org/wiki/Bild_Lilli_doll*.
3.*The West Wing*, season 3, "Women of Qumar."

While Barbie may inspire girls to go into certain careers, let's hope prostitution isn't one of them. Real life prostitutes don't end up with wealthy businessmen like Vivian Ward (Julia Roberts) did with Edward Lewis (Richard Gere) in the film *Pretty Woman* (1990). Though most prostitutes can't sing like Anne Hathaway, a more realistic portrayal of the profession is found in the character Fantine in *Les Misérables*, who dies in poverty from tuberculosis, leaving her daughter, Cosette, an orphan.[4]

Amazingly, though, the Bible tells of several prostitutes whose stories have happy endings because they become significant characters in God's story. As we'll see in this chapter, love, Old Testament style, sometimes involves prostitutes or even a pimping patriarch, and yet God is able to redeem their tragic stories and use them to accomplish his purposes.

Before looking at Old Testament laws and stories involving prostitutes, I need to comment on the topic of this book. Friends often ask me, "What are you working on now?" and when I tell them, "Prostitutes and polygamists in the Old Testament," some of them reply with a note of cynicism, "Sex. That'll sell." As my family and I were driving to a movie recently, the topic of *Game of Thrones* came up, and I commented (after not reading the books or viewing the show), "The only reason *Game of Thrones* is popular is because of the sex and violence."[5]

To this, my son Noah responded, "Sounds like your books, Dad."[6]

I get no respect. To friends (and family) who think that I'm the type of author who simply prostitutes himself by writing books about sexy topics, let me point out that my first book was about Deuteronomistic redaction, the dynasty of Jehu (2 Kings 9–10), and dynastic succession.[7] Enough said?

---

4. Anne Hathaway played Fantine in the 2012 film version of *Les Misérables*.

5. The TV series *Game of Thrones* is produced by HBO (2011–current) based on the fantasy novel series A Song of Ice and Fire by George R. R. Martin. The first book is titled *A Game of Thrones* (New York: Bantam, 1996).

6. I discuss the violence of God in *God Behaving Badly* (93–113).

7. As dissertations go, it's more readable than most. David Lamb, *Righteous Jehu and His Evil Heirs: The Deuteronomist's Negative Perspective on Dynastic Succession* (Oxford: Oxford Univ. Press, 2007).

Prostitution Prevention

Lest one think that because God is graciously able to redeem women who have fallen into "the world's oldest profession," he somehow approves of this vocational decision, let's start by looking at the relevant biblical laws. At the risk of stating the obvious, the Bible thinks prostitution is wrong, and this perspective is clearly stated in the three Old Testament laws that address the subject.

> Do not profane your <u>daughter</u> by making her a **prostitute**, lest the *land* fall into **prostitution** and the *land* become full of depravity.
>
> — Leviticus 19:29

> When the <u>daughter</u> of a priest profanes herself through **prostitution**, she profanes her father; she shall be burned to death.
>
> — Leviticus 21:9 NRSV

> None of the <u>daughters</u> of Israel shall be a cult **prostitute**, and none of the sons of Israel shall be a cult **prostitute**.
>
> — Deuteronomy 23:17

We can start by making three observations about these laws. First, at least for priestly daughters, prostitution was a capital offense ("burned to death"), as were other sexual sins discussed elsewhere in this book, including adultery, rape, incest, and homosexuality (Lev. 20:10–13; Deut. 22:25). To our modern sensibilities, these offenses do not seem to warrant a death sentence; the punishment doesn't seem to fit the crime.[8] However, we don't see any clear examples of these sentences being meted out in the Old Testament. We could, therefore, understand these laws to essentially be saying that these sins warrant

---

8. Wenham helpfully notes that capital punishment in the Pentateuch represents "a maximum not a minimum," and he discusses the principles behind these punishments at length. Gordon J. Wenham, *The Book of Leviticus* (Grand Rapids, Mich.: Eerdmans, 1979), 278–86.

death, similar to when the apostle Paul states that "the wages of sin is death" (Rom. 6:23). While God smites people for a variety of reasons in Scripture,[9] the text never records divine smiting for explicit acts of prostitution, incest, or homosexuality. (If you're thinking, "What about Sodom?" good question, but wait until chapter 7.) Nor does God ever punish people for *not* performing capital punishment against perpetrators of these sexual sins.

Second, as the third of these laws clearly states, both female and male prostitution is forbidden. These laws don't just target women, and not all prostitutes are female. While most of the prostitutes mentioned in the Old Testament were women (this chapter will discuss in-depth two of the more famous ones: Tamar and Rahab), at various points during the monarchy, male cult prostitution thrived, forcing reforming rulers like Jehoshaphat and Josiah to attempt to eradicate it (1 Kings 14:24; 15:12; 22:46; 2 Kings 23:7).

Third, prostitution prevention is the responsibility not merely of the individual prostitute but of the entire community. These laws describe how prostitution negatively affects (profaning or depraving) not just the prostitute but also the parents and the land. According to these laws, parents share responsibility for the situations leading to prostitution. All three of these laws speak of "daughters," and Leviticus 19 is directly addressed not to the prostitute but to the parent who is supposed to prevent it. Because the land represents not merely the actual ground but also the people of the land, the entire community has a vested interest in preventing prostitution.

The biblical understanding of corporate responsibility for prostitution prevention takes seriously the complicated nature of the various sociological factors that can lead to this type of lifestyle, which can include poverty, abuse, oppression, and addiction. For prostitutes to move out of this lifestyle, acceptance, support, and community involvement will be essential.

---

9. See *God Behaving Badly*, chapter 2, for a discussion of God's smiting anger.

Prophets, Priests, and Prostitutes?

While perhaps not playing as significant a role in Israel's story as prophets and priests (although "Prophets, Priests, and Prostitutes" is quite catchy), a surprising number of prostitutes are major characters in the narrative of the Old Testament. Not all are portrayed negatively, and several are portrayed surprisingly positively.

Two judges are associated with prostitution: Jephthah's mother was a prostitute (Judg. 11:1) and Samson patronized one (Judg. 16:1), and in both of these contexts, the text doesn't explicitly condemn their behavior. Whereas after Dinah's rape by Shechem, her brothers take drastic measures so their sister is not treated like a prostitute, so clearly they perceive a stigma associated with the profession (Gen. 34:31).

When two prostitutes ask for wisdom from King Solomon to determine who is the true mother of the one remaining child and he declares, "Bring me a sword," apparently to chop the living infant in half, the two prostitute single mothers aren't condemned for their occupation (1 Kings 3:16–28). During the time of Israel's kings, prostitutes were deemed worthy of an audience with a king, and the one who offered to sacrificially give up her infant boy to save his life is cast in a favorable light. The prophet Hosea is called by God to marry the prostitute Gomer as an illustration of what God has experienced with his faithless "wife" Israel. However, the book of Hosea provides few details about Gomer's life, and she is mentioned by name only once in the book (Hos. 1:3). But before discussing the prostitutes Tamar and Rahab, we need to look at Abraham, who was more than just a faithful forefather.

Abraham: The Pimping Patriarch

During a period of famine in the land of Canaan, Abraham decides to take his family on an extended vacation to Egypt, where they have food to spare. While in Egypt the faithful patriarch, who boldly trusted

God when he left Haran to come to Canaan, becomes the unchivalrous patriarch who would rather endanger his wife than himself.

> When he was about to enter Egypt, he said to Sarai his **wife**, "I know that you are a woman beautiful in appearance, and when the Egyptians see you, they will say, 'This is his **wife**.' Then they will kill me, but they will let you live. Say you are my sister, that it may go well with me because of you, and that my life may be spared for your sake." When Abram entered Egypt, the Egyptians saw that the woman was very beautiful. And when the princes of Pharaoh saw her, they praised her to Pharaoh. And the woman was taken into Pharaoh's house. And for her sake he dealt well with Abram; and he had sheep, oxen, male donkeys, male servants, female servants, female donkeys, and camels.
>
> But the LORD afflicted Pharaoh and his house with great plagues because of Sarai, Abram's **wife**. So Pharaoh called Abram and said, "What is this you have done to me? Why did you not tell me that she was your **wife**? Why did you say, 'She is my sister,' so that I took her for my **wife**? Now then, here is your **wife**; take her, and go."
>
> — Genesis 12:11–19

Abraham's wife Sarah, despite being sixty-five years old, is still quite attractive, the matriarchal equivalent of Helen Mirren. Abraham fears that as they enter the land of Egypt, he will be killed by Pharaoh so that he could add Sarah to his harem.[10] Abraham, therefore, hatches a plot to deceive Pharaoh by claiming Sarah is not his wife but his sister. Since Sarah is actually his half sister, the daughter of his father, but not his mother (Gen. 20:12), he is not being completely dishonest. (We'll revisit this story in chapter 6.) However, the primary relational reality for Abraham and Sarah is not that of siblings but of spouses, so the message to Pharaoh was deceptive.

---

10. Technically, their names are still Sarai and Abram here, since they aren't changed until Genesis 17, but I'll still call them Sarah and Abraham.

For Abraham, the ruse allows his life to be preserved, and he is richly rewarded by Pharaoh with animals and servants. Presumably, one of the female servants given to Abraham was Hagar, who plays a significant role later in the narrative, as we saw in chapter 3 (Gen. 16:1). For Abraham, handing his wife over to Pharaoh was a highly lucrative transaction. He left Egypt a much richer man than he entered it. We have a name for someone who profits by trafficking women for sex. A pimp.[11] Thus, we can call Abraham the pimping patriarch.

Sarah: The Power Rape Victim

While the plan worked out great for Abraham, it didn't turn out as well for Sarah. She joined Pharaoh's harem. Yahweh says nothing in Egypt to the patriarch he had just commissioned (Gen. 12:1–3), but to get Pharaoh's attention, he sent plagues on the Egyptians (foreshadowing the plagues in the book of Exodus). Pharaoh somehow figures out that the plagues are because of Sarah, so he confronts and rebukes Abraham and forces him to leave.

Did Pharaoh actually have sex with Sarah? While the text isn't clear, tragically for Sarah it appears that he did. Pharaoh himself states that he took her as his wife (Gen. 12:19). Gordon Wenham thinks that since Yahweh afflicted Pharaoh with great plagues (Gen. 12:19), adultery was committed.[12]

Shockingly, similar versions of this incident are repeated in two other texts within the Patriarchal narratives (Genesis 20; 26). In episode two of the my-wife-is-my-sister trilogy, after Abraham has repeated his pimping patriarch routine by lying to King Abimelech of Gerar about his "sister" Sarah (and my wife thinks I'm a bad husband?), Abimelech makes it clear that he didn't touch Sarah. The Pharaoh of Genesis 12 makes no such claim, adding further support to the idea that Sarah was fully his wife. While it was not uncommon

---

11. The "pimping" language was used independently by my wife, Shannon, and my seminary's president, Frank James, to describe Abraham's behavior here, so I take that as a sign from God that I should use it.

12. Gordon J. Wenham, *Genesis 1–15* (Waco, Tex.: Word, 1987), 289.

for rulers to have harems in the world of the ancient Near East, from our perspective, Sarah appears to have been a victim of a power rape (see also chapter 5).

Abraham's behavior in Egypt is appalling, the antithesis of chivalry as he commanded his wife to "take one for the team" (i.e., for him). We aren't sure what Pharaoh would have done if he had known they were actually married, but even if Abraham's assumption was accurate, a courageous patriarch would have risked his life for his beloved instead of throwing her under the bus to save his own skin.

How did Sarah feel about this whole episode? We don't know, since she doesn't say a word, but we can guess. I was teaching this story at church recently, and as we read the passage aloud I assigned four people to read the parts of the narrator, Abraham, Pharaoh, and Sarah. After the reading, I asked "Sarah" how she felt. She was clearly frustrated. "I didn't even get to speak." Sarah's silence is deafening.

Thus, Sarah was a victim of Pharaoh's lust and Abraham's cowardice. For Abraham, his fear of Pharaoh overcame his faith in Yahweh. God had just promised to make his name great and to bless all the families of the earth through him (Gen. 12:1–3). If he had been able to trust God's promise, he wouldn't have needed to worry about anything in Egypt.

While Abraham seemed to be concerned only about his own well-being, profiting as he handed over his beautiful wife Sarah to Pharaoh for sex, God was looking out for her. In stark contrast to her pathetic husband, God was chivalrous and defended her by getting the attention of Pharaoh in Genesis 12 with plagues and of Abimelech in Genesis 20 with a dream. It is possible that God protected her from sex in Genesis 12, but the text seems to suggest otherwise.

Why does God not protect fully women in situations of trafficking, prostitution, and rape?

I do not know. But I do know that God calls both men and women to act like he does here for Sarah and defend women who are being sexually exploited.

Like father, like son—Isaac concludes the my-wife-is-my-sister trilogy by lying about his wife Rebekah to ... King Abimelech of Gerar again. What must Abimelech have thought about the morality of those patriarchs? Fortunately, Abimelech figured out that Rebekah was Isaac's wife before anything happened.

Abraham's narrative includes a tragically parallel couplet of twisted spouse-swapping incidents:

- In Genesis 12, Abraham allowed the Egyptian Pharaoh to take Sarah as his wife.
- In Genesis 16, Sarah allowed Abraham to take the Egyptian Hagar as his wife.

While Abraham is looked to elsewhere in Scripture as a model of faithfulness (Gal. 3:6; Heb. 11:8–19), the influence he has on his wife and his son when it comes to marriage is clearly negative.

Yahweh called Abraham to bless the nations (Gen. 12:1–3). However, because of his lack of faithfulness, the first thing he does is essentially to curse them by bringing plagues on Egypt. And yet God still worked through the pimping patriarch to bless the nations. Jesus, the descendant of Abraham, blessed all the families of the earth, including pimps and prostitutes, since he came to save not the righteous but the sinners (Mark 2:17).

Associations with prostitutes run in Abraham's family, as we'll see next with his great-grandson Judah.

Tamar: The First Woman of the New Testament

The first woman mentioned in the New Testament isn't Mary the mother of Jesus or Elizabeth the mother of John the Baptist. When you realize that Matthew begins with a genealogy, you might think the first woman of the New Testament would be the first woman of the Old Testament, Eve. Nope. Well, then, surely it has to be one of the wives of the patriarchs, Sarah, Rebekah, or Leah. Nope, nope, nope. The first woman of the New Testament is Tamar (Matt. 1:3).

What did Tamar do to be put in such an exalted position alongside

Jesus, David, and Abraham? She acted like a prostitute. Shocking perhaps, but not after we take a look at Genesis 38, the story of Tamar, the pious prostitute.[13]

Judah, the son of Jacob, the son of Isaac, the son of Abraham, had three sons: Er, Onan, and Shelah (Gen. 38:1–5). Er was wicked, so God killed him. To forgive is divine, but Er was too human. Onan also was wicked, so God killed him too.

We know nothing about the nature of Er's evil, but Onan's wickedness was related to his unwillingness to impregnate Tamar, his brother Er's Canaanite wife, in order that Er's ancestral lineage would continue. This practice, also called levirate marriage, which we discussed in the previous chapter, may seem bizarrely creepy to us today. ("Would you like to sleep with your sister-in-law while she's in mourning over the death of your brother?" "No, but thanks for asking.") But apparently it was normal back then, and it was later codified (Deut. 25:5–6). Onan was willing to "go in to" Tamar, but he was reluctant to impregnate her because it would dramatically reduce his own inheritance, so he spilled his seed on the ground. (Onan's solitary claim to fame is that his behavior here prompted the term *onanism*, defined as either masturbation or *coitus interruptus*, if you prefer Latin medical terminology.[14] I think this association is an appropriate penalty for Onan.) Onan's sexual exploitation of Tamar, using her for his sexual pleasure while denying her the dignity of motherhood, was so displeasing to Yahweh that Onan was killed (Gen. 38:8–10).

After Onan's death, Judah promised Tamar that his youngest son, Shelah, would take on the duty that Onan was unwilling to do, but she would need to wait until he got older. (Can you imagine waiting years to have sex with an underaged relative? Is it possible to get even creepier?) But as the time came, Judah did nothing to unite Shelah and

---

13. For a spiritually insightful discussion of the story of Tamar, see Carolyn Custis James, *Lost Women of the Bible* (Grand Rapids, Mich.: Zondervan, 2005), 103–19. For an engaging academic discussion of Tamar's story, see Yairah Amit, "The Case of Judah and Tamar in the Contemporary Israeli Context: A Relevant Interpolation," in *Genesis: Texts@contexts* (Minneapolis: Fortress, 2010), 213–20.

14. See *http://www.merriam-webster.com/dictionary/onanism*.

Tamar, presumably because he blamed Tamar for the deaths of his two older sons and he didn't want lightning to strike thrice. However, the text makes it clear that Er and Onan were killed for their wickedness and Tamar was innocent of their deaths. But some men like Judah will always find a way to blame a woman.

From Widow Tamar to Prostitute Tamar

Shortly after Judah's wife dies, when Tamar realizes Judah isn't going to make Shelah perform his sibling duty, Tamar hatches a plot. With a Barbiesque wardrobe change, she transforms from Widow Tamar to Prostitute Tamar and goes to sit near the town gate where she knows Judah will soon be traveling. She assumes that her father-in-law, because he's been a widower for a while, might be "in the mood" for love (boys will be boys — immoral, that is). Assuming she's a prostitute and not a sneaky daughter-in-law, because she's wearing a veil, he propositions her and promises to pay the standard fare. The going price for a trick back then was one goat. (Some things never change.) Since he has just spent his last goat, he instead gives her his signet ring, cord, and staff as collateral, until he is able to put the goat in the mail. This exchange would be comparable today to someone giving away their driver's license and credit cards.[15] To hand over all his valuables to a stranger like this must have meant he was *really* in the mood. After Judah returns home, he sends a friend with the goat to retrieve his things, but the "prostitute" is gone, so he gets to keep the goat for next time.

Meanwhile, his daughter-in-law has also returned, quickly changing from Prostitute Tamar back to Widow Tamar. A few months later, Tamar's pregnancy test tells her that her scheme has succeeded ("It's blue!"), and later we discover that she is carrying twins (to be named Perez and Zerah). Her father-in-law is not as excited to hear about the pregnancy.

---

15. See also the discussion of Robert Alter regarding this transaction in *The Five Books of Moses: A Translation with Commentary* (New York: Norton, 2004), 217.

> About three months later Judah was told, "Tamar your daughter-in-law has been immoral. Moreover, she is pregnant by immorality." And Judah said, "Bring her out, and let her be burned." As she was being brought out, she sent word to her father-in-law, "By the man to whom these belong, I am pregnant." And she said, "Please identify whose these are, the signet and the cord and the staff." Then Judah identified them and said, "*She is more righteous than I*, since I did not give her to my son Shelah." And he did not know her again.
>
> — Genesis 38:24–26

The text doesn't provide us with Judah's rationale for his judgment, but several factors suggest that he is merely taking advantage of the situation to solve his problem of the deadly daughter-in-law. First, Judah doesn't hesitate to pronounce death and orders it to take place instantly, seen more clearly in the Hebrew as his judgment consists of only two words: "take-her-out," "that-she-be-burned."[16] Second, even though death sentences were not typically performed without multiple witnesses (Num. 35:30; Deut. 17:6–7), in his haste Judah doesn't ask for any witnesses or any evidence. Third, the death by burning that he decrees was the most severe form of capital punishment — the Prostitute Burning Law of Leviticus 21:9 (in the future from the perspective of Genesis 38) was reserved only for the daughters of priests.

While we, the readers, know who the father actually is, Judah has no reason to suspect it is his child. Thus he is pronouncing death not only on his daughter-in-law but also on his own sons/grandsons — his own heirs. As the death sentence for sexual immorality is ironically proclaimed by the man who impregnated her, we see the clear negative consequences of the "curse" of Genesis 3:16: "he shall rule over [her]."

Judah has no qualms about hypocritically declaring death for her even though he is also guilty of "immorality" like his daughter-in-law. He has no reason to expect that his crime will be exposed, since no one else knows about it except for the mysterious woman (and his

---

16. Ibid., 219.

goat-delivering friend … and the goat). But then, in a dramatic twist of fate for Judah, Tamar reveals that the father is none other than the owner of the signet, cord, and staff. ("Hmm, those look familiar …") I'd love to have seen the expression on Judah's face then. At this point, Judah has a crucial choice to make, either to cover up or to come clean.

Tamar the Pious Prostitute

Fortunately for Tamar and for the sake of his soul, Judah chooses to come clean. Not only that but he boldly declares, "She is more righteous than I." *He got that one right.*

Judah was unrighteous because he was selfishly attempting to fulfill his sexual desires. Tamar, however, was righteous because she was cleverly trying to honor her deceased husband Er, to continue his lineage, and to provide for herself so she wouldn't need to resort to prostitution as a lifestyle. She was a pious prostitute.

Some may think Tamar's one-time gig as a prostitute would disqualify her from the ranks of the pious, and yet Scripture refers to Tamar exclusively in favorable terms. At the end of the book of Ruth, the people of Bethlehem pronounce a blessing on Ruth that recalls the fruitfulness of Tamar, mother of Perez (Ruth 4:11–12). David's daughter Tamar was presumably named after his distant ancestor (2 Samuel 13; we'll discuss her in chapters 5 and 6), which would mean that she was perceived as someone worthy of honoring in this manner. And, as we noted a few pages earlier, Tamar was the first woman of the New Testament. Tamar has a highly positive biblical legacy.

Over twenty years ago, when I was working with kids in a summer youth program, I remember meeting a ten-year-old girl named Tamar. I thought, "Why would someone name their child after a prostitute or a rape victim?" Now I know why. Because the Tamars in the Bible were impressive women. David's family named a daughter after Tamar, the pious prostitute.

Tamar the Undervalued

One can argue not only that Tamar was righteous but also that she is one of the most undervalued people, not just women, in the entire Old Testament, since her actions appear to be the catalyst for a massive transformation in the life of Judah, the ancestor of David and Jesus.

Let's review Judah's story. He gets off to a good start, since his name means "praise" (Gen. 29:35), but it quickly goes downhill from there. Judah is absent from the text until he proposes the scheme to his brothers to sell Joseph to slave traders (Gen. 37:27).[17] He raises a batch of wicked sons. He deceives his daughter-in-law Tamar about giving her his third son, Shelah. He propositions Tamar, thinking she's a prostitute. He condemns her for sexual immorality when he is the only one guilty of that particular crime. All of his deeds so far in the text are evil — until clever Tamar sends back his signet ring, cord, and staff, prompting him to declare that she is more righteous than he. Apparently, his interaction with pious Tamar somehow transforms him.

Judah again disappears from the narrative of Genesis until, after Joseph has orchestrated events to test whether his brothers will repeat the sell-your-youngest-brother-into-slavery routine, Judah offers to become a slave in place of his youngest brother, Benjamin (Gen. 44:18–34). The person most responsible for Joseph's enslavement is thus also the person most responsible for Joseph's fraternal reconciliation. After his encounter with Tamar the pious prostitute, Judah morphs from being a prostitute-frequenting, slave-trading brother into a self-sacrificing, volunteer-to-be-enslaved brother. Tamar's significance in the biblical narrative cannot be overstated. Perhaps that's why she's the first woman of the New Testament.

And curiously, when it comes time for a father's final blessing, Jacob declares that not the oldest, Reuben, and not the favorite, Joseph, but the

---

17. Against the argument that Judah is looking out for his younger brother by suggesting the sale of Joseph, see the comments of Robert Alter (*Five Books of Moses*, 211). Judah's primary concern here is not the welfare of Joseph but the welfare of Judah. He wants to profit from the transaction.

transformed slave-trader, Judah, is the one deemed worthy to receive a promise of an eternal royal dynasty (Gen. 49:10), a declaration which points forward first to David (2 Samuel 7), but then ultimately to Jesus, specifically to his royal genealogy, where Tamar appears first among females. Tamar's twins, Perez and Zerah, are the only twins mentioned in the genealogy, but Tamar wasn't the only prostitute. The great-great-great-great-grandson of Judah, Salmon (pronounce the *l*, not like the fish), was the husband of yet another sexually scandalized Canaanite "grandmother" in Jesus' family tree, the prostitute named Rahab.

Rahab: The Faithful Prostitute

I was in the middle of a spiritual retreat at St. Andrew's Abbey, a Benedictine monastery in the desert of California. I visited the gift shop to purchase a book for my fiancée, Shannon, something to communicate what I thought of her.

A card? *Not enough.*

A ceramic saint? *Not our tradition.*

A crucifix? *Not romantic.*

I couldn't find anything that would send the right message, but I persisted. I was confident that I would find the right gift eventually. Finally, I came across a book that I thought would be perfect: *Harlots of the Desert.*[18]

Shannon wasn't impressed. I guess it didn't send the right message.

I thought she might like this story of penitent women from the early history of the church since she loved the story of Rahab in particular and had even given a first-person narrative talk on the life of this Canaanite prostitute. But for some reason she didn't think it was romantic. (I did admit in chapter 2 that I'm not good with romance.)

But before talking about Rahab, we need to rewind the tape a bit to give some important background to her story from Numbers 13–14. Forty years earlier, Moses sent twelve spies into the land. Things

---

18. Benedicta Ward, *Harlots of the Desert: A Study of Repentance in Early Monastic Sources* (Kalamazoo, Mich.: Cistercian, 1987).

didn't go so well; ten of the spies thought that the grasshopperesque Israelites wouldn't do well in battle with the giantesque Canaanites. Two of the spies, Caleb and Joshua, were confident based on their experience in Egypt, where their God had just delivered them from the greatest military power on the planet, but the people chose to believe the pessimistic ten, not the optimistic two. Their refusal to listen to Moses, Caleb, and Joshua prompted God to make them do forty years of "laps" in the wilderness.

After the death of Moses, Joshua is promoted from spy to national leader and the Israelites finally approach the land again. When Joshua has a chance to send out spies to check out the land, he decides to send only two. Perhaps if only Joshua and Caleb had been sent last time, they would have been established in the land already.

> And Joshua the son of Nun sent two men secretly from Shittim as spies, saying, "Go, view the land, especially Jericho." And they went and came into the house of a **prostitute** whose name was **Rahab** and lodged there. And it was told to the king of Jericho, "Behold, men of Israel have come here tonight to search out the land." Then the king of Jericho sent to **Rahab**, saying, "Bring out the men who have come to you, who entered your house, for they have come to search out all the land." But the woman had taken the two men and hidden them. And she said, "True, the men came to me, but I did not know where they were from. And when the gate was about to be closed at dark, the men went out. I do not know where the men went. Pursue them quickly, for you will overtake them." But she had brought them up to the roof and hid them with the stalks of flax that she had laid in order on the roof. So the men pursued after them on the way to the Jordan as far as the fords. And the gate was shut as soon as the pursuers had gone out.
>
> —Joshua 2:1–7

Why did these two unnamed spies visit the home of the prostitute? Let's assume (perhaps naively) that they weren't looking to give her any business, because Israelite men would never do that (except for Samson ... and Judah ... and probably a few others). (Notice, I displayed unusual restraint in not making a joke about the name of the city they were sent from.) Unlike the story of Tamar in Genesis 38, no reference is made of Rahab actually plying her trade in Joshua 2, but she was apparently sufficiently established in this particular ancient profession that it was how she was identified. She wasn't Rahab the daughter of Bob or Rahab from the south side of Jericho (the baddest part of town) but Rahab the prostitute, which is what the text repeatedly calls her (Josh. 2:1; 6:17, 25).

The narrative provides no details regarding her sexual behavior, but it goes into depth describing how she risked her life for these two spies. She accepts them into her home. (She did have some experience with hospitality.) She baldly lies to the king's soldiers about the spies' whereabouts, cleverly convincing the soldiers to leave quickly so they won't lose the trail. Her behavior so far warrants death, as treason is typically considered a capital offense, but what she does next is even more dramatic.

> Before the men lay down, she came up to them on the roof and said to the men, "I know that the **LORD** has given you the land, and that the fear of you has fallen upon us, and that all the inhabitants of the land melt away before you. For we have heard how the **LORD** dried up the water of the Red Sea before you when you came out of Egypt, and what you did to the two kings of the Amorites who were beyond the Jordan, to Sihon and Og, whom you devoted to destruction. And as soon as we heard it, our hearts melted, and there was no spirit left in any man because of you, **for the LORD your God, he is God in the heavens above and on the earth beneath**. Now then, please swear to me by the **LORD** that, as I have dealt kindly with you, you also will deal kindly with my father's house, and give me a sure sign that you will save alive my father and mother, my brothers and sisters, and all who belong to them, and deliver our lives

from death." And the men said to her, "Our life for yours even to death! If you do not tell this business of ours, then when the **LORD** gives us the land we will deal kindly and faithfully with you."

— Joshua 2:8–14

Both sides faithfully fulfill their obligations. Rahab doesn't reveal their business, and they rescue her and her family from destruction (Joshua 6), but let's examine what she says to the two spies here. She gives them exactly what they are looking for, insider information about the status of the population of Jericho — the city is living in fear and dread. She reminds them of how their God delivered them forty years earlier from the Egyptians and more recently from the Amorites on their way to Jericho. She expresses confidence in their God's ability to defeat the residents of the land. She empowers them to return in faith. She utters one of the most dramatic monotheistic declarations in Scripture: "He is God in the heavens above and on the earth beneath."

While ten Israelite men who had witnessed God's dramatic deliverance in Egypt distrusted God's ability to achieve a repeat performance in Canaan, one Canaanite woman who had merely heard secondhand reports of those events *knew* that God had already given them the land. The audience was small, but her minisermon delivered to these two men, which was then relayed to Joshua and the nation, was far more effective than the message delivered forty years earlier to the nation from Caleb and Joshua.

Perhaps that's why Rahab's New Testament legacy is so shockingly favorable. The book of James mentions only three individuals from the Old Testament (not counting God); I call them the big three: the (pimping) patriarch Abraham, the prophet Elijah, and the prostitute Rahab (James 2:21, 25; 5:17). While Rahab's actions are the focus in James, her faith is the focus in Hebrews. The faith of this prostitute gave faith to the nation, and her faithful example caused her to be enshrined in the "Hall of Faith" in Hebrews 11. The military hero of the conquest, Joshua, is omitted from the chapter, but Rahab is given her own verse, alongside Abraham, Moses, Samuel, and her great-great-grandson

David (Heb. 11:31; Matt. 1:5–6), as well as her great-great-great ... grandson Jesus (Heb. 12:2; Matt. 1:5–16).

Jesus and the Loving Prostitute

While it may not be surprising for a guy with prostitutes in his family tree, Jesus' ability to attract people with sexual issues was always controversial. Let's look at how he interacts with one particular woman over dinner at the home of Simon, an important religious leader.

One of the Pharisees asked him to eat with him, and he went into the Pharisee's house and reclined at the table. And behold, a **woman** of the city, who was a *sinner*, when she learned that he was reclining at table in the Pharisee's house, brought an alabaster flask of ointment, and standing behind him at his feet, weeping, she began to wet his feet with her tears and wiped them with the hair of her head and kissed his feet and anointed them with the ointment. Now when the Pharisee who had invited him saw this, he said to himself, "If this man were a prophet, he would have known who and what sort of **woman** this is who is touching him, for she is a *sinner*." And Jesus answering said to him, "Simon, I have something to say to you." And he answered, "Say it, Teacher."

"A certain moneylender had two debtors. One owed five hundred denarii, and the other fifty. When they could not pay, he cancelled the debt of both. Now which of them will love him more?" Simon answered, "The one, I suppose, for whom he cancelled the larger debt." And he said to him, "You have judged rightly." Then turning toward the **woman** he said to Simon, "Do you see this **woman**? I entered your house; you gave me no water for my feet, but she has wet my feet with her tears and wiped them with her hair. You gave me no kiss, but from the time I came in she has not ceased to kiss my feet. You did not anoint my head with oil, but she has anointed my feet with ointment. Therefore I tell you, her *sins*, which are many, are forgiven — for she loved much. But he who is forgiven little, loves little." And he said to her, "Your *sins* are forgiven." Then those who were at table with him began to say among themselves, "Who is this, who even forgives *sins*?" And he said to the **woman**, "Your faith has saved you; go in peace."

— Luke 7:36–50

Not long after Jesus arrives at Simon the Pharisee's house, an uninvited guest shows up, a woman of the city who is widely known as a sinner, not exactly the sort of person Jesus' host appreciates sharing Jesus with. Any hope of her disappearing discretely is dashed as she begins to wash Jesus' feet with her tears, wiping them with her hair, kissing them with her lips, and anointing them with her anointment. Talk about intimate; if he weren't Jesus, one might wonder if something sexual is going on. Jesus says she loves much.

Is she a prostitute? I think so for three reasons.[19]

First, she's certainly got both the skills (feet kissing) as well as the tools (alabaster anointment) for the art of making a man feel special; she appears to be an experienced seductress. While one might think Jesus would be embarrassed about all this intimate attention (if something like this were to happen in a church today, people would freak out), he emphasizes how the tear washing, hair wiping, feet kissing, and ointment anointing point out the host's lack of hospitality.

Second, her sinful status is obvious as both the narrator and the Pharisee call her a "sinner" and Jesus refers to her sins as "many." It's hard to imagine another type of sin that this woman could be associated with that would have more severe negative associations than that of a prostitute. (Perhaps tax fraud?)

Third, elsewhere in the Gospels, tax collectors are lumped interchangeably with "sinners" (Matt. 9:10–11; 11:19) and "prostitutes"

---

19. The text doesn't explicitly identify her as a prostitute, but most commentators assume that is what the term "sinner" (*hamartōlos*) implies. Kenneth E. Bailey states, "The natural and nearly universal assumption is that she is a prostitute," *Jesus through Middle Eastern Eyes* (Downers Grove, Ill.: InterVarsity, 2008), 244.

(Matt. 21:31–32), suggesting that the terms "sinners" and "prostitutes" are synonymous. In Matthew 11:19, Jesus is accused of being a friend of tax collectors and sinners. In Matthew 21:31–32, he says that prostitutes and tax collectors will enter the kingdom of God before the religious leaders, which sounds similar to the message he gives in Luke 7 to this particular religious leader.

I think she was a prostitute. So what do we learn about Jesus from this story of the forgiven prostitute?

Jesus honors women, even ones dishonored by men. While Simon's judgmental attitude toward her may not seem as bad as Abraham pimping his wife or Judah plotting to kill his pregnant daughter-in-law, Jesus still rebukes Simon severely. Simon thinks Jesus isn't a prophet, but Jesus addresses his unspoken critique, making it clear that he is a prophet since he knows she has a big debt. Simon may not believe this sort of woman should touch the feet of prophets, but Jesus believes that this particular woman can teach even religious leaders a lesson about hospitality. Jesus uses this forgiven prostitute's shocking deeds of intimate hospitality (tears-and-hair foot washing, foot kissing, ointment anointing) to highlight Simon's lack of hospitality (no foot washing, no kissing, no anointing).

The story of this forgiven prostitute who loved much fits a broader gospel pattern where women who are typically marginalized by men are praised and honored by Jesus.[20] Therefore, men who are followers of Jesus will not dishonor, but will honor and learn from women who want to be forgiven by Jesus, which leads to the next point we learn about Jesus.

Jesus forgives anyone who seeks him, even prostitutes. Jesus had a reputation of being associated with tax collectors, sinners, and prostitutes (Luke 15:1–2). Why were these types of people drawn to Jesus? Because Jesus wasn't repulsed by them, he wasn't embarrassed to eat with them, and he wasn't afraid to be touched by them. He was

---

20. Examples of this phenomenon where Jesus honors unexpected women include the woman who anointed Jesus' feet at Bethany (Mark 14:3–9), the widow who gave a mite (Mark 12:41–44), the widow of Zarephath (Luke 4:25–26), and the widow who persisted with the unjust judge (Luke 18:1–8).

friendly with them, which shouldn't surprise us since he had prostitute grandmothers (Tamar and Rahab) and pimping/adulterous and polygamous grandfathers (Abraham and David). Associations with people involved in sexual scandals ran in his family. But most importantly, he forgave them, just like he did this woman with many sins who loved much. Just like Rahab, her faith saved her, so Jesus told her to go in peace.

Learn, Tell, Pray

The stories of the four women we've looked at in this prostitution chapter all end positively. Sarah was delivered by God with supernatural plagues from Pharaoh's harem and became the mother of Isaac. Tamar was declared to be more righteous than Judah and became the mother of twins. Rahab was welcomed into the family of Israel and became the mother of Boaz. While we know nothing about her family, the loving prostitute departed in peace, a forgiven woman.

While these stories have happy endings, most prostitute stories don't end positively but, as we said at the beginning of this chapter, are more like Fantine's in *Les Misérables*, a death in poverty. If that reality isn't enough to make you lose hope, the astronomical number of prostitutes scattered throughout the world might do the trick. In their bestselling 2009 book, *Half the Sky*, Kristof and WuDunn estimate that approximately three million women and girls are enslaved in the sex trade, and more females are being sent into brothels annually in the twenty-first century than African slaves were sent into plantations in the eighteenth or nineteenth centuries.[21] The problem of global prostitution and sex trafficking is one of staggering proportions.

What can be done? We need to start by remembering that the God who redeemed Tamar, Rahab, and the loving prostitute of Luke 7 is still at work calling sinners of all kinds to himself. And we should recall from our discussion about prostitution prevention that helping

---

21. Nicholas D. Kristof and Sheryl WuDunn, *Half the Sky: Turning Oppression into Opportunities for Women Worldwide* (New York: Knopf, 2009), 10–11.

people out of the sex trade industry will require community involvement. Here are three things everyone who is concerned about the global prostitution problem can do.

Learn about prostitutes in the Bible and about sex trafficking in the world. Don't ignore these amazing stories of biblical women with a sexually scandalous past. The biblical authors included them in Scripture to teach us lessons in surprising ways. We learn about piety from Tamar, faith from Rahab, and love from the forgiven prostitute. Investigate, support, and get involved in ministries like International Justice Mission (IJM) that rescue victims of the sex trade and bring criminals to justice.[22] In response to a desire to learn more about IJM, I recently read a book by its president, Gary Haugen, titled *Just Courage,* in which I learned about Donaldina Cameron, who worked for forty-five years in San Francisco's Chinatown and rescued over three thousand girls from forced prostitution.[23]

What do you do with what you're learning? *Tell stories.* Talk about Tamar, Rahab, and the loving prostitute at church and at work, at home and at school, because many people can learn a lot about piety, faith, and love from prostitutes. If you use social media networks, post, tweet, or blog about IJM or other ministries that you learn about as you read, investigate, and travel. I have only one personal story of interacting with a sex worker, and I told the story of Sandy, who went by the name Domino, in the acknowledgments, so I won't repeat it here, but I did devote a chapter of this book to the topic.[24]

While learning and telling stories, remember to *pray.* Pray for people like Donaldina, who minister to people in the sex trade industry. Jesus says the harvest is plentiful, but laborers are few, so pray that the Lord of the harvest raises up laborers (Luke 10:2). But beware, you may become the answer to your own prayers.

Not far from where I live is a show bar where the "dancers" often do more than dance. People from several local churches began meeting

---

22. International Justice Mission's website: *http://www.ijm.org/.*
23. Gary Haugen, *Just Courage: God's Great Expedition for the Restless Christian* (Downers Grove, Ill.: InterVarsity, 2008), 86–87.
24. See also *God Behaving Badly* (174–75).

in a church a few blocks from the lounge to pray for their community. Two elderly ladies from the prayer group went out on a prayer walk one night to intercede for the needs of their neighborhood, and they ended up in the parking lot of the bar. The owner of the establishment saw them standing there and asked them what they were doing. They apparently didn't look like either patrons or employees.

The two ladies told the owner they were praying for their neighbors and the local businesses, which was not what he had expected. After chatting for a few minutes, he ended up telling them about his own health problems. He had liver cancer. He invited them to come into the lounge, which was not what they had expected, and there they prayed for him and his cancer, that God would heal him.

Thus began a relationship between the Gentlemen's Club and the church ladies. The ladies continued to ask for prayer requests from the owner and the dancers. Eventually, a nice wooden box was put in the dancers' dressing room with a sign — Prayer Requests — and the church ladies regularly came and collected requests from the dancers. Again, not expected, but a small, hopeful sign in a dark place.

Learn from the church ladies, pray for sex workers who live near you, and get involved in a ministry that provides support to help people get out of the lifestyle.

Pelagia: A Harlot of the Desert

While I was writing this chapter in March of 2014, I visited Jerusalem for the first time. As we were walking down the slope of the Mount of Olives, our Jewish guide Nathan pointed out an old tomb along the path. When he mentioned that this tomb was traditionally associated with a prostitute named Pelagia, my curiosity was piqued.[25]

---

25. For an academic discussion of the Jewish, Christian, and Muslim traditions associated with this tomb, see Ora Limor, "Sharing Sacred Space: Holy Places in Jerusalem between Christianity, Judaism, and Islam," in *In Laudem Hierosolymitani: Studies in Crusades and Medieval Culture in Honour of Benjamin Z. Kedar*, ed. Iris Shagrir, Ronnie Ellenblum, and Jonathon Riley-Smith (Burlington, Vt.: Ashgate, 2007), 227–29.

After returning from Israel, I was pleased to discover that the ancient tale of Pelagia the courtesan from Antioch is retold (translated from the Latin original) in the book I gave Shannon before our wedding, *Harlots of the Desert*.[26] I'll retell it here.

In front of the door of the church in Antioch a group of bishops is gathered to meet in the open air. As the monk-bishop Nonnus is speaking to his esteemed colleagues, Margaret, the most famous actress of the city, rides past on a donkey, beautifully adorned in "nothing but gold, pearls and precious stones"[27] and followed by an entourage of boys and girls who were enthralled by her beauty. All the other bishops immediately turn away, averting their eyes from the sexual temptation. Nonnus, however, fixes his eyes upon her and gazes at her intently as she goes by.

After she leaves, he turns to the bishops and speaks the unexpected: "Were you not delighted by such beauty? . . . I was very greatly delighted and her beauty pleased me very much."[28] That's apparently not what the bishops were thinking, so they are silent. But then he speaks about this woman that pious people shun, and he makes her into a positive example. He exhorts his brothers to notice how focused she is on making herself beautiful in order to please her lovers, in contrast to many in the church who are far less focused on pleasing their "immortal Bridegroom," who had blessed them in more ways than the woman's lovers had. When he is alone, Nonnus prays fervently for the beautiful actress.

On Sunday, the same Margaret, who had never before visited a church, happens to come and hears Nonnus preach. She is instantly convicted of her sins and lifestyle and, after returning home, sends a letter to Nonnus describing herself as a "sinner and a disciple of the devil" and asking for the mercy of God, who "came not for the

---

26. Ward, *Harlots*, 57–75. Ward includes an English translation from the Latin of *The Life of Saint Pelagia the Harlot*. Ward helpfully acknowledges that "literary figures emerge from the story of Pelagia which are perhaps not identical with the historical persons who gave rise to the tales" (58).
27. Ibid., 67.
28. Ibid.

righteous but for the salvation of sinners." In her humble request that the pious monk-bishop would be willing to meet with a sinner like herself, she mentions how Jesus was willing to meet with "the harlot in Samaria at the well" (John 4).[29]

He agrees to meet, but not privately, only publicly with a group of other bishops present. She rushes to the church and begs to be baptized while seizing the feet of Nonnus and "washing them with her tears and wiping them with the hair of her head."[30] *Now, where have we seen that before?*

In her confession before Nonnus and his gang of bishops, she informs them that although her stage name is Margaret (which means pearl), her parents had named her Pelagia. After her baptism by Nonnus, she begins going by that name. Pelagia then declares that all her possessions — her gold, silver, precious stones, and pearls — should be given to the church. And then the proceeds from the sale are given to orphans, widows, and the poor.

Eight days after her baptism, Pelagia mysteriously departs from Antioch and moves to Jerusalem, to a cave outside the city on the slope of the Mount of Olives, where she lives dressed as a monk in simplicity and prayer for the rest of her life.

Her ancient biographer, the Deacon James, concludes her story with these words:

> May the life of this harlot, this account of total conversion, join us to her and bring us all to the mercy of the Lord on the day of judgment, to whom be glory and power and honour to the ages of ages. Amen.[31]

---

29. I wouldn't call her a harlot just because she went to the well at noon; a polygamist, but not a prostitute (see chapter 3).
30. Ward, *Harlots*, 70.
31. Ibid., 75.

CHAPTER 5

RAPISTS AND ADULTERERS

Rape in the Military

In a *Doonesbury* comic from 2013, a balding military officer with a big nose is sitting behind a desk looking down at his papers.[1] Without looking up, he says to the blond female sergeant standing in front of him, "What do you want Wheeler?" They are both wearing fatigues.

Sergeant Wheeler replies, "I'd like to report a crime, colonel. As required, I am reporting it through my chain of command." A map of Afghanistan is behind her head.

He says, "What's the crime?"

She says, "I was raped by a superior officer."

The colonel finally looks her in the eye. "Who's the alleged perpetrator?"

Wheeler: "You, sir, as you know."

The colonel looks back down to his papers. "Not credible. Dismissed."

---

1. Garry Trudeau, *Doonesbury* (December 8, 2013), *http://doonesbury.slate.com/strip/archive/2013/12/8.*

The scene changes to Sergeant Wheeler speaking to two other females in their quarters with bunk beds in the background after she has told them about her interaction with the colonel.

With a look of horror, one of the women says to Wheeler, "What?"

The other says, "Seriously?"

Wheeler responds, "Welcome to the military, ladies."

Rape is never funny, always tragic, and yet in this strip Garry Trudeau somehow exposes the outrageous irony of an officer deciding the credibility of a rape case when he was in fact the perpetrator, which is currently the situation in the US military.[2] According to an anonymous survey, twenty-six thousand American soldiers, mostly women, were victims of sexual assault in 2012.[3]

While I'm sure the vast majority of people who serve in the military do so with honor and respect toward the other gender, these numbers should appall us. The US military has yet to figure out how to address this rape epidemic. There are way too many Sergeant Wheelers out there.

Rape on Campus

While writing this chapter, I opened our mailbox one day and pulled out the most recent *Time* magazine and read the cover: "Rape: The Sexual Assault Crisis on American Campuses."[4] The campus statistics, like the military ones, are shocking. One out of five females is a victim of sexual assault during college, but colleges want to cover up rape statistics, since high numbers reflect negatively upon the school.

---

2. On military rape, see Mark Thompson, "The Military's Latest Rape-Case Mess: A Sexual Assault Case Reveals an Unbalanced Military Justice System," *Time*, September 16, 2013, *http://content.time.com/time/magazine/article/0,9171,2151156,00 .html*.

3. Survey results in Ruth Rosen, "The Invisible War against Rape in the US Military," *History News Network*, March 24, 2014, *http://hnn.us/article/155049*.

4. See Eliza Gray, "Rape: The Sexual Assault Crisis on American Campuses," *Time*, May 26, 2014, *http://time.com/100542/ the-sexual-assault-crisis-on-american-campuses/*.

One of the related articles in *Time* was titled "Redefining Rape." The problem of defining and legislating rape today is that what constitutes rape can be difficult to determine, as many cases become "he said," "she said" scenarios. Sex usually happens with no witness.

If the armed forces and universities struggle to negotiate the gray areas between coerced and consensual sex in the twenty-first century, we shouldn't be surprised that in the ancient world of the Bible there are some gray areas that don't make sense to us. While the military and the university worlds seem to be ignoring these issues, more than twenty-five hundred years ago the Old Testament addressed these issues head on by recording both stories of rape and laws judging adulterers and rapists.

Rape and Adultery in the Old Testament

As a male, I feel uncomfortable talking about rape. Forgive me if and when I am insensitive. To readers who are rape victims, all I can say is that I'm really, really sorry. In *God Behaving Badly*, I discuss why God smites people in anger. Seriously, why doesn't God just smite all the rapists?

I do not know.

While I feel uncomfortable, I still need to discuss the issue of rape in a book about non-ideal sexual behavior in the Old Testament. The Old Testament talks about rape as it both narrates and punishes it.

So in this chapter we'll see what God's Word has to say about rape. I hope this chapter not only helps people get a better biblical understanding of a difficult subject but also is a small step toward healing for rape victims and, perhaps, even rapists.

Alongside the issue of rape, I'll also talk about the issue of adultery. Why combine these two topics? Because the Bible does. In the Old Testament, the rape and adultery laws appear together. And for at least one biblical story, scholars debate whether the sexual encounter involved rape or adultery. But to help us distinguish between rape and adultery, we'll first need to define the relevant terms.

Consent and Coercion

While these terms may already be familiar, I'll still define them, starting with terms of volition.

- *Consensual sex* means both sides choose it; it's voluntary. In the Bible, all sex should be consensual and should occur in the context of a marriage between a man and a woman.
- *Coercive sex* means one side is being forced into sex by the other; it's not voluntary. Coercion can involve violence or merely threats of violence, humiliation/shame, professional rewards for agreement or punishments for refusal, etc.

Sex should always be consensual, but as the rape crises in the military world and in the college world reveal, consent and coercion are not always clear-cut. If we put totally consensual sex on one end of a spectrum and totally coercive sex on the other end, there is still a large gray area in the middle.

On the consensual side of the spectrum we find the standard forms of seduction and romantic inducements, including flowers, chocolates, sexy attire, or small quantities of alcohol. ("Candy is dandy, but liquor is quicker.") On the coercion side of the spectrum we find manipulation, verbal and physical abuse, and large quantities of alcohol (a major factor in college rapes).

Next we need to define sex acts not between a husband and a wife.[5] *Adultery* is consensual sex between two people who aren't married to each other, but at least one of whom is married to someone else. *Rape* is coercive, involuntary, forced sex, usually upon a woman by a man. As we look at the relevant laws we'll ask, what is the nature of the sexual act taking place? Is it adultery, rape, or some type of seduction in the gray area in the middle? More could be said about these terms, but now let's turn to the laws.

---

5. The Bible doesn't directly address rape in the context of marriage.

Adultery Laws: Adulterers Finish Last

In the film *42* (2013), Dodgers owner Branch Rickey (Harrison Ford) calls from New York to wake up his manager Leo Durocher (Christopher Meloni) in Los Angeles to ask him if he would have a problem managing Jackie Robinson, who would become the first black major league baseball player. Rickey quotes the Bible to encourage Durocher to take on Robinson.

Durocher finally asks, "Is he a nice guy?"

Rickey replies, "No, if you mean soft."

Durocher is pleased and replies with his signature line: "Good, nice guys finish last."

In the background Rickey hears a woman. Rickey concludes the conversation with a warning: "The Bible has a thing or two to say about adultery as well." Yes, it does.

Whether or not they are legally posted in courtrooms, classrooms, or bathrooms, most of us are familiar, although not as familiar as we think we are, with the Ten Commandments. Among the Big Ten, number seven makes it clear what God thinks about adultery.

> You shall not commit adultery.
>
> —Exodus 20:14; Deuteronomy 5:18

Terse and to the point. No adultery. There's not much to discuss, except that unlike some of the other adultery laws focused on men, this one speaks generally to both men and women. What the seventh commandment doesn't do is prescribe any punishments for the two guilty parties, but Leviticus takes care of that.

> If a man commits adultery with the wife of his neighbor, both the adulterer and the adulteress shall surely be put to death.
>
> —Leviticus 20:10

As I mentioned in the previous chapter, adultery and other sins like prostitution don't seem to us today to deserve capital punishment. The severity of the punishment makes it clear that God wants to uphold the ideal of one man and one woman for marriage. To paraphrase the adulterer Leo Durocher, "Adulterers finish last."

Adultery Laws: Every Adulterer Must Get Stoned

Deuteronomy 22:22–29 includes a series of four laws related to sexual sins associated with adultery and rape.[6] Four specific scenarios are mentioned, each beginning with an "if." All four cases speak of a man as one of the partners, but his female partner is different (a wife, an engaged virgin, an engaged young woman, and a non-engaged virgin). In each scenario, a sexual sin has occurred, and the law pronounces consequences. We'll first look at two laws that address adultery, then two laws that address rape. (In case you weren't sure, the expression "lying with" means having sex.)

Adultery Law 1 involves consensual sex with another man's wife.

"If a **man** is found *lying with* the <u>wife</u> of another **man**, both of them shall die, the man who *lay* with the <u>woman</u>, and the <u>woman</u>. So you shall purge the evil from Israel."

— Deuteronomy 22:22

Adultery Law 2 involves consensual sex with an engaged[7] virgin in the city.

If there is a betrothed [or "engaged"] <u>virgin</u>, and a **man** meets her in the city and *lies with her*, then you shall bring them both out to the gate of that city, and you shall stone them to death with stones, the <u>young woman</u> because she did not cry for help though she was in the city, and the man

---

6. See the helpful discussion of these adultery and rape laws in Paul Copan, *Is God a Moral Monster?* (Grand Rapids, Mich.: Baker, 2011), 118–19.

7. While betrothal and engagement are not technically identical, since they are comparable, I will speak of a woman as "engaged" even though the English translation may say "betrothed." See also David L. Baker, *Tight Fists or Open Hands? Wealth and Poverty in Old Testament Law* (Grand Rapids, Mich.: Eerdmans, 2009), 104.

because he violated his neighbor's **wife**. So you shall purge
the evil from your midst.

—Deuteronomy 22:23–24

As we said before, there are two problems when it comes to legislating sex crimes. First, sex usually takes place in private with no witnesses; and second, it can be difficult to determine whether the sex was consensual or coercive.

Both of these cases seem to involve consensual sex. In Adultery Law 1, they are found, so if coercion was a factor, then it would have come out. In Adultery Law 2, they are in a city where she could have cried out for help if she were being raped, but she didn't. These two cases both have the same penalty as the law of Leviticus 20:10: death. The second one spells out the execution method: stoning. ("Every adulterer must get stoned.") And notice there is no distinction between punishment for the man and the woman, which suggests that in these hypothetical scenarios, they both freely chose to be involved sexually, which is not the case in the next two laws.

Rape Laws: Green Acres Is Better Than Sex in the City

Rape Law 1 involves an engaged woman in the country.

But if in the open country a **_man_** meets a **young woman** who is betrothed, and the **_man seizes her and lies with her_**, then only the **_man_** who lay with her shall die. But you shall do nothing to the **young woman**; she has committed no offense punishable by death. For this case is like that of a **_man_** attacking and murdering his neighbor, because he met her in the open country, and though the betrothed **young woman** cried for help there was no one to rescue her.

—Deuteronomy 22:25–27

Rape Law 2 involves a non-engaged virgin.

> If a _**man**_ meets a **virgin** who is not betrothed, and _**seizes**_
> _**her and lies with her**_, and they are found, then the _**man**_
> who lay with her shall give to the father of the young woman
> fifty shekels of silver, and she shall be his wife, because he
> has violated her. He may not divorce her all his days.
>
> — Deuteronomy 22:28–29

In contrast to the previous two adultery cases, which involve consensual sex, these two rape cases involve coerced sex, and therefore, the consequences are different. The coercion technique in the rape cases involves the use of force ("seizes her").

While the distinction between the engaged "virgin" (_betulah_) in Adultery Law 2 and the engaged "young woman" (_na'arah_) in Rape Law 1 doesn't appear to be significant, the different location is. The woman in the city could have called for help, but the woman in the country could not have been heard even if she screamed. In both cases the man dies, but while the engaged woman of the city shares the fate of her partner, the engaged woman of the country is spared. In terms of the result for the woman, _Green Acres_ is better than _Sex in the City._[8]

While a person could not normally be sentenced to death merely on the testimony of one witness (Deut. 17:6), it appears that isn't the case here and that this female victim is given the benefit of the doubt against her male rapist (which is not true today in the US military or on college campuses). Since the rape occurred in the country, there were no other witnesses. Wright states, "The court should accept what could only be the woman's testimony in the matter and assume her innocence."[9] Tigay states, "She is given the benefit of the doubt and presumed to have called for help."[10] While determining what constitutes rape can

---

8. _Green Acres_ was a US TV show on CBS (1965–1971) about a glamorous woman (Eva Gabor) who had to leave her beloved New York City because her husband (Eddie Albert) wanted to run a farm. _Sex in the City_ was a US TV show on HBO (1998–2004) about the sexual escapades of four women in New York City. I watched many reruns of the former, and about thirty minutes of the latter. _Green Acres_ was much better than _Sex in the City._

9. Christopher J. H. Wright, _Deuteronomy_ (Peabody, Mass.: Hendrickson, 2003), 244.

10. Jeffrey H. Tigay, _Deuteronomy_ (Philadelphia: Jewish Publications Society, 1996), 207.

be difficult, this Old Testament rape law gives the benefit of the doubt to the woman. In this respect, ancient Israelite law is shockingly more progressive than current US laws.

The fact that we don't see any examples of a death sentence for adultery being meted out in the Old Testament, and that in the New Testament Jesus shows mercy toward the woman caught in adultery (more on her later), suggests this punishment is meant to make a strong statement, while still allowing for compassion and forgiveness toward repentant adulterers. Lest we forget, the bad news of the Bible is that everyone, not just adulterers and rapists, deserves death, but the good news of the Bible is that followers of Jesus escape our deserved punishment.

Rape Laws: Marrying Your Rapist?

In Rape Law 1 he dies and she lives, but in Rape Law 2 they get married. What's up with that? To understand why the consequences are so dramatically distinct, we need to look at how these two laws differ. While Rape Law 1 is on the far end of the coercion spectrum, Rape Law 2 is more in the middle, more gray. There are three significant differences between these two laws.

First, in Rape Law 1, she's already engaged, but in Rape Law 2, she's not engaged yet, so marriage is only an option in Law 2. But who'd want to marry a rapist? Great question; we're still working on that.

Second, even though the ESV translation uses the same English word *seizes* in these two rape laws, the Hebrew words are different. In Rape Law 1, a more violent word, *chazaq*, is used. The word *chazaq* is twice used in other rape contexts, when the Levite "forces" his concubine outside, where she is raped (Judg. 19:25), and when Amnon "seizes" Tamar and rapes her (2 Sam. 13:11). In Rape Law 2, the word *tapas* is used, which isn't as strong as *chazaq* and can mean just "hold" or "take." In a close parallel to this law, the word *tapas* is used when Mrs. Potiphar "takes hold of" Joseph (Gen. 39:12), but Joseph is able to resist her grasp. It's more subtle than Rape Law 1. The fact that *chazaq* is used elsewhere in contexts of violent coercive rape, while *tapas* is used elsewhere in a context of an unsuccessful seduction, suggests that the crime perpetrated in Rape Law 2 is different from the one perpetrated in Rape Law 1, less violent and more resistible.

Third, in Rape Law 2, the couple is "found" (*matsa'*), but there's no mention of the couple being found in Rape Law 1, where the female victim presumably was the one who exposed the rape. The couple in the Adultery Law 1 was also "found" and since that case was consensual, it again suggests the scenario of Rape Law 2 was less coercive than that of Rape Law 1.[11]

If we imagine a spectrum, with consensual sex on the far left and coercive sex on the far right, the two adultery laws of Deuteronomy 22 would be on the far left consensual side, Rape Law 1 would be on the far right coercive side, and Rape Law 2 would still be on the coercive side, but shifted toward the middle, since it includes less coercive elements and more seduction elements.

It's impossible to describe precisely what hypothetical scenario Rape Law 2 is meant to be addressing or what we should label it, but using contemporary terminology, it sounds like it could entail seduction, date rape, or statutory rape.

While it still may not make sense to us, there are strong cultural reasons for the couple described in Rape Law 2 to get married for the sake of the rape victim. I discuss why this law makes sense in its ancient Near Eastern context in more depth in *God Behaving Badly* (61–64), so here I'll only point out that the victimized woman would probably never marry in that society, which means she likely ends up destitute or as a prostitute. A marriage to this man, whom she probably already knows, would provide her with necessary security. And she would have more security than her peers, since he can never divorce her. The story of the rape of Tamar by Amnon adds further support to these points (2 Sam. 13:1–19; see also chapter 6).

Before concluding this section, we need to briefly recall the

---

11. There are several striking parallels between Rape Law 2 and the seduction law of Exodus 22:16–17, adding further support for the idea that the context of Rape Law 2 is less coercive than that of Rape Law 1.

discussion in chapter 3 regarding foreign prisoners-of-war wives, specifically that rape was forbidden in those contexts. Foreign women in the time of ancient Israel had more legal protection than American women serving in the US military today. Something is not right.

Seduction, Adultery, and Rape in the Old Testament

Before looking in more depth at two rape stories, I'll first briefly mention other incidents of seduction, adultery, and rape in the Old Testament. The following incidents I discuss in other contexts: both Hagar (see chapter 3) and Sarah (see chapter 4) may have been victims of power rapes; Lot offered his daughters to be raped (see *God Behaving Badly*, 60–61, 63–64); Tamar was raped by Amnon (see chapter 6); and Lot was also raped by his daughters (see chapter 6).

The Old Testament includes a few more relevant incidents. As we just noted, Mrs. Potiphar attempted to seduce and force Joseph into sex, but he refused (Gen. 39:7–20). After Shechem raped Dinah, the daughter of Jacob, he attempted to woo her to marry him, but her brothers had other plans (Genesis 34). When Absalom seized the throne from his father David, his advisor Ahithophel recommended that he "go in" to his father's concubines to make a public statement (2 Sam. 16:21–22). While all of these stories have their own challenges, there isn't time to look at them here except to observe that the Old Testament doesn't avoid talking about seduction, adultery, and rape.

The Gang Rape of the Levite's Concubine

Perhaps the most disturbing story in all of Scripture is the rape of the Levite's concubine (Judges 19).[12] To give some background, a Levite

---

12. For an insightful, close academic reading of the story of the rape of the Levite's concubine, see Phyllis Trible, *Texts of Terror: Literary-Feminist Readings of Biblical Narratives* (Philadelphia: Fortress, 1984), 64–91. Eric Seibert includes an interesting

and his concubine wife are returning from Bethlehem to their home in the hill country of Ephraim. After multiple delays, they stop in the city of Gibeah for the night. In Gibeah, initially no one offers them a place to stay until an old man finally extends hospitality to them. As we join the story, they are all having a good time after dinner, until disaster strikes.

> As they were making their hearts merry, behold, the men of the city, **worthless** fellows, surrounded the house, beating on the door. And they said to the old man, the master of the house, "Bring out the man who came into your house, that we may know him." And the man, the master of the house, went out to them and said to them, "No, my brothers, do not act so **wickedly**; since this man has come into my house, do not do this **vile** thing. Behold, here are my **virgin daughter** and his **concubine**. Let me bring them out now. Violate them and do with them what seems good to you, but against this man do not do this **outrageous** thing." But the men would not listen to him. So the man seized [*chazaq*] his **concubine** and made her go out to them. And they knew her and abused her all night until the morning. And as the dawn began to break, they let her go. And as morning appeared, the woman came and fell down at the door of the man's house where her master was, until it was light. And her master rose up in the morning, and when he opened the doors of the house and went out to go on his way, behold, there was his **concubine** lying at the door of the house, with her hands on the threshold. He said to her, "Get up, let us be going." But there was no answer. Then he put her on the donkey, and the man rose up and went away to his home. And when he entered his house, he took a knife, and taking hold [*chazaq*] of his **concubine** he divided her,

---

nonviolent reading of the violence against women texts; see Eric Seibert, *The Violence of Scripture: Overcoming the Old Testament's Troubling Legacy* (Minneapolis: Fortress, 2012), 129–46.

limb by limb, into twelve pieces, and sent her throughout all the territory of Israel. And all who saw it said, "**Such a thing** has never happened or been seen from the day that the people of Israel came up out of the land of Egypt until this day; consider it, take counsel, and speak."

—Judges 19:22–30

Sometimes sexual encounters are gray. This one was not. The heinous crime perpetrated against this woman goes off the spectrum, way beyond merely coerced rape.

She was abandoned, discarded, and sacrificed by her host.

She was gang raped, tortured, and murdered by her countrymen.

She was betrayed, dismembered, and scattered by her husband.

All the men who should have protected her deserted and exploited her. Phyllis Trible concludes that, of all the characters in Scripture, "this woman is the most sinned against."[13]

Scholars note the many parallels between this rape and the story of Lot, who offers his daughters to the men of Sodom to protect the angels he is hosting (Genesis 19). (We'll talk more about Sodom in chapter 7.) I'll point out three striking similarities between the two stories here involving the guests, the men, and the host.

First, the guests from out of town almost spend the night in the town square but are offered hospitality by a man who was not originally from the city (Gen. 19:2; Judg. 19:17–21). In a world without motels, hanging out in the town square waiting for a host was the ancient Israelite version of booking a room through Expedia or Orbitz.

Second, the men of the city surround the home of the host and demand that the guest(s) be brought out, so they can "know" them (Gen. 19:5; Judg. 19:22). In the laws set between these two incidents, God makes it clear how strangers should be treated, commanding his people to welcome, not exploit, foreigners (Exod. 22:21; 23:9).

Third, the host refuses the mob's offer, saying "my brothers, do not act so wickedly" and makes a counter offer involving virgin daughter(s) instead (Gen. 19:7–8; Judg. 19:23–24). Hospitality is generally a

---

13. Trible, *Texts of Terror*, 81.

good thing, but here, the hospitality goes berserk. What kind of a dad offers his daughter to a mob?

The big difference between Genesis 19 and Judges 19 is the fate of the females. In Genesis, Lot's daughters are spared when the angels blind the men of the city; however, in Judges, when her husband seizes her and tosses her outside, the concubine is brutally ravished to death. I don't know which is more disturbing, a father who offers his daughter or a husband who offers his wife to be gang-raped, but both actions are evil and cowardly (like Abraham handing over Sarah to Pharaoh in Genesis 12).

Does the Bible Think Gang Rape Is Okay?

One of the most troubling aspects of this highly disturbing story is the fact that there doesn't appear to be a clear condemnation in the text. Does the Bible think gang rape is okay?

No, it does not. While we might prefer something more obvious ("their deeds were evil in the sight of the LORD"), Old Testament narratives often allow readers to come to their own conclusions. Despite the lack of an explicit condemnation, the message about the evilness of these men is communicated clearly in three ways.

First, the text states that the rapists themselves are worthless. Second, their actions are described as wicked, vile, and outrageous — and uniquely so in the history of Israel. Third, their city, Gibeah, is compared to Sodom. Sodom was so wicked it was destroyed. While Sodom was known for its incredible wickedness, Gibeah appears to be more depraved. And Gibeah was destroyed in a civil war, prompted by the national outrage against this heinous crime (Judges 20–21). The text is clear. Gang rape is wickedly vile.

I hate the story of the Levite's concubine. If I wrote the Bible, it wouldn't have made the cut. And I'm not the only one who avoids this disturbing story. Despite Paul's clear teaching that "all Scripture is inspired by God and profitable for teaching" (2 Tim. 3:16 NASB), no one seems to teach on it. Why is this story in the Bible?

Even though I don't like it, I still think it's good that God's Word includes stories like the rape of the Levite's concubine. Tragically, rape happens. And catastrophically, violent gang rape happens. While we may want to ignore it, we shouldn't. Unlike the academy and the military, the Bible doesn't ignore stories of rape. What will it take for our country to be so outraged by the brutal rapes taking place right now in the military and on college campuses that we do something — like the people during the time of the judges? Civil war probably isn't a good idea, but drastic steps need to be taken.

David Rapes Bathsheba?

When people ask about my first name, I respond, "I'm named after the most famous murderer and adulterer in history." After studying his story more carefully, I think I'm going to need to replace *adulterer* with *rapist*.

The story of David and Bathsheba is one of the most familiar in the Bible.

> In the spring of the year, the time when kings go out to battle, David sent Joab, and his servants with him, and all Israel. And they ravaged the Ammonites and besieged Rabbah. But David remained at Jerusalem.
>
> It happened, late one afternoon, when David arose from his couch and was walking on the roof of the king's house, that he saw from the roof a **woman** bathing; and the **woman** was very beautiful. And David **_sent_** and inquired about the **woman**. And one said, "Is not this Bathsheba, the **daughter** of Eliam, the **wife** of Uriah the Hittite?" So David **_sent messengers_** and took her, and she came to him, and he lay with her. (Now she had been purifying herself from her uncleanness.) Then she returned to her house. And the **woman** conceived, and she **_sent_** and told David, "I am pregnant."
>
> — 2 Samuel 11:1–5

In regard to the dynamic of what actually took place between David and Bathsheba, there is significant textual ambiguity. Did it involve adultery, seduction, or rape? I took a poll on my blog, asking, "Who's to blame?"[14] Here are the results (with 104 responses):

- 1 percent answered, "Bathsheba; she tempted him."
- 69 percent answered, "David; she had no choice."
- 27 percent answered, "Both; she wanted it, he wanted it."
- 3 percent answered, "Someone else."

My poll was not exactly a scientific study, but it was still interesting to see how people assign the blame. Most think David was responsible, but almost a third think it was mutual. In the classic film *David and Bathsheba* (1951), starring Gregory Peck and Susan Hayward (I'll let you figure out who played whom), she knows that he is watching her bathe and hopes that he will be enticed; Hollywood blames both.

Some scholars think that Bathsheba wanted to be seen while bathing as a plot to seduce David; therefore, she bears a significant part of the blame, but I couldn't disagree more.[15] Many commentators use the word *adultery* to describe what occurred, implying that Bathsheba consented to the affair and was, therefore, somewhat to blame, but it wasn't adultery.[16] Most scholars are reluctant to use the term *rape*, but

---

14. Part 1: *http://davidtlamb.com/2013/10/29/david-and-bathsheba-whos-to-blame-2-sam-11/*; part 2: *http://davidtlamb.com/2013/11/11/david-or-bathsheba-whos-to-blame-part-2/*.
15. Scholars who blame Bathsheba for seducing David include E. Randolph Richards and Brandon J. O'Brien, *Misreading Scripture with Western Eyes: Removing Cultural Blinders to Better Understand the Bible* (Downers Grove, Ill.: InterVarsity, 2012), 121–22, and George G. Nichol, "The Alleged Rape of Bathsheba: Some Observations on Ambiguity in Biblical Narrative," *Journal for the Study of the Old Testament* 73 (1997), 43–54. Popular author Liz Curtis Higgs considers Bathsheba a "really bad girl" for seducing David; Liz Curtis Higgs, *Really Bad Girls of the Bible* (Colorado Springs: WaterBrook, 2000), 123–61.
16. Several commentators who describe the affair as adultery include Robert Alter, *Ancient Israel: The Former Prophets: Joshua, Judges, Samuel and Kings* (New York: Norton, 2013), 481; David G. Firth, *1 and 2 Samuel* (Downers Grove, Ill.: InterVarsity, 2009), 417. Alexander Izuchukwu Abasili ("Was It Rape? The David and Bathsheba Pericope Re-examined," *Vetus Testamentum* 61 [2011], 1–15) argues that Bathsheba did not seduce David, but that their affair was not rape according to the Bible. I agree with Abasili's first point, but not his second.

a few scholars think that David may have raped Bathsheba and he was totally to blame.[17] I think she was raped.

Bathsheba: Innocent until Proven Guilty

A painting by Jean Bourdichon (1457–1521) depicts a nude, seductive Bathsheba right outside the window of King David. (He's wearing a gold crown.)[18] She's glancing back at him with an alluring, inviting, "come hither" look. While biblical themed art always involves interpretation, there is little in the text to support this one.

Despite the assumptions of scholars, artists, and screenwriters who blame Bathsheba, the text gives no clues about Bathsheba's motivation, so we should be careful about assigning blame.[19] She was beautiful, but the Bible doesn't command ugliness. Bathsheba did take a bath, but there is nothing wrong with bathing. Most people I know are pro-bath.

In terms of her bath, Firth makes two valid points: first, she may have just been using a bowl, and second, she wasn't necessarily naked.[20] In terms of her trying to be seen, Gordon and Anderson both argue that we should not assume she was aware of the "royal voyeur," since there is no textual support for the idea.[21] I agree.

As we think of David's home, we may envision an expansive European palace where a commoner would have to try hard to be seen by a noble. But David's palace was no Versailles. Houses inside walled cities like Jerusalem weren't far apart. I visited Jerusalem a few months ago and walked through the City of David in the area where the king

17. Richard M. Davidson calls David's act a "power rape" in "Did David Rape Bathsheba? A Case Study in Narrative Theology," *Journal of the Adventist Theological Society* 17 (2006), 81–95.

18. Jean Bourdichon, *Bathsheba Bathing*, http://commons.wikimedia.org/wiki/File:Jean_Bourdichon_(French_-_Bathsheba_Bathing_-_Google_Art_Project.jpg.

19. For a detailed discussion of the textual traditions involving Bathsheba and her characterizations in these texts, see Sara M. Koenig, *Isn't This Bathsheba?* (Eugene, Ore.: Pickwick, 2011).

20. Firth, *1 and 2 Samuel*, 417.

21. Robert P. Gordon, *I and II Samuel: A Commentary* (Waynesboro, Ga.: Paternoster, 1986), 253; A. A. Anderson, *2 Samuel* (Dallas: Word, 1989), 153.

may have had his home; the dwellings were right next to each other. It wouldn't have been hard for David to see his neighbors from his roof.

In a US courtroom today, a person charged with a crime is innocent until proven guilty, but apparently that's not the case with Bathsheba. It's not illegal to be pretty, not illegal to bathe (naked or not), not illegal to be seen, and not illegal to be the victim of rape. There is absolutely no evidence to convict Bathsheba of anything. With David, however, it's a different story.

David: Guilty as Charged

While nothing in the text implicates Bathsheba, the text places all the blame on my beloved namesake.[22] First, let's look at David's role in the narrative of the actual affair (2 Sam. 11:1–5).

David took all the initiative to instigate the affair. He saw her, he inquired about her, he sent messengers to get her, he took her, and he laid with her. The only thing she did was to agree to come when ordered by her sovereign. She would have no reason to suspect something sexual was afoot but probably thought David was going to give her news, most likely bad news, about the fate of her husband, Uriah, which is exactly what happens later in the story after David has him killed (2 Sam. 11:26).

David had the power; Bathsheba was powerless. He was a man; she was a woman. He was a king; she was a commoner. David had armies of soldiers and servants at his disposal to do his bidding. Bathsheba had only her husband to protect her from the king, but Uriah was away serving the king at the front, where David should have been, instead of lusting after his neighbor's wife.

---

22. The name David may mean "beloved."

Don't Blame the Lamb!

Now let's look at how the text assigns blame in the context of the parable told by Nathan the prophet to David the king (2 Sam. 11:27b–12:7a). All of the blame is placed entirely on David.

> But the thing that David had done displeased the LORD. And the LORD sent Nathan to David. He came to him and said to him, "There were two men in a certain city, the one **rich** and the other **poor**. The **rich man** had very many flocks and herds, but the **poor man** had nothing but one **little ewe lamb**, which he had bought. And he brought it up, and it grew up with him and with his children. It used to eat of his morsel and drink from his cup and lie in his arms, and it was like a **daughter** to him. Now there came a traveler to the **rich man**, and he was unwilling to take one of his own flock or herd to prepare for the guest who had come to him, but he took the **poor man's** **lamb** and prepared it for the man who had come to him." Then David's anger was greatly kindled against the **man**, and he said to Nathan, "As the LORD lives, the **man** who has done this deserves to die, and he shall restore the lamb fourfold, because he did this thing, and because he had no pity." Nathan said to David, "You are the **man**!"
>
> — 2 Samuel 11:27b–12:7a

Yahweh blames David, not Bathsheba. Throughout the narrative thus far there's been no mention of God, but he finally steps in to pronounce judgment on David. The narrator states that what David did displeased the LORD. There's no mention of Bathsheba's behavior provoking divine displeasure. Yahweh's displeasure prompts him to send his prophet.

Nathan blames David, not Bathsheba. In the parable that Nathan tells David, the rich man (David) bears all the guilt for "taking" (*laqach*) the sheep (Bathsheba) of his poor neighbor (Uriah) to slaughter and serve for his guest (2 Sam. 12:4). Tellingly, the same verb for "take" (*laqach*) is used three times in this narrative to describe what David did to Bathsheba (2 Sam. 11:4; 12:9–10).[23] While several scholars want to put some of the blame on Bathsheba, the parable makes this idea seem tragically comical. It's not the ewe's fault that it got slaughtered. Blame David, not the Lamb!

David blames David, not Bathsheba. After listening to Nathan's parable, David declares, "The man who did this deserves to die," and in doing so, he unwittingly pronounces his own death sentence. Nathan drives the message home to his king by revealing the identity of the rich man: "You are the man!"

Fortunately for David's soul, he responds to Nathan's pronouncement humbly by repenting: "I have sinned against the LORD" (2 Sam. 12:13), and Nathan tells him that Yahweh has forgiven him and he won't die. But their child will die.

Yahweh, Nathan, and David all essentially declare that David deserves death for what he did, but they are silent on the subject of Bathsheba's punishment. Deuteronomy 22 prescribes death for both the man and the woman in an instance of consensual adultery, but death only for the man in an instance of coerced rape (Rape Law 1). If what happened between David and Bathsheba was adultery, then Bathsheba also deserved death, and the text should make that clear, as it does for David. Since the text places all the blame on David and states that only he deserves death, based on Deuteronomy 22, we should assume that what took place was rape.

What was the punishment for David's rape of Bathsheba? That his wives would be raped, which happened when his son Absalom "went in" to his concubines during his attempted coup (2 Sam. 16:21–22). We don't have space here to discuss this problematic punishment, but in the spirit of "an eye for an eye," this sentence adds support to the idea that David raped Bathsheba.

The argument that the sexual encounter between David and Bathsheba was mutual because it occurred in the city and she did not

---

23. The ewe is compared to a daughter, which establishes another link between the sheep and Uriah's wife, since the Hebrew word for daughter is *bat*, which is the first part of Bathsheba's name (*bat-sheva'*).

cry out for help ignores the severe power differential involved. If she were to have cried out, which one of David's soldiers was going to rush in and stop the commander-in-chief in the moment of passion? Look what happened to Uriah.

This Little Light

Both before and after the rape, numerous messengers, servants, and soldiers went between the royal palace, Bathsheba's house, and the war front serving as virtual accomplices to David's crime (2 Sam. 11:2–6, 12, 14, 22). These messengers had to suspect what was going on, and yet none of them tried to stop David until finally Yahweh sent Nathan. Often rapes and sexual abuse could have been stopped sooner if the people who suspect something had intervened.

In 2009, Christa Brown published her story of sexual abuse by her pastor while she was a teenager, *This Little Light: Beyond a Baptist Preacher Predator and His Gang.*[24] Numerous aspects of her story are highly disturbing. The abusive pastor frequently used Scripture to manipulate Christa into sexual encounters. He read Song of Solomon to her, and since he was already married, he reminded her of all the Old Testament polygamists to justify their relationship. But perhaps most troubling of all, once charges of sexual abuse came out against several Baptist pastors, the denomination protected the perpetrators, not the victims. If you or someone you know was abused, seek professional help from a therapist or counselor and learn about the process of healing.[25]

The military, the academy, and sometimes even the church are reluctant to blame the man in contexts of sexual abuse, but the Bible is not. Even when a rape involves the leader of the nation, the

---

24. Christa Brown, *This Little Light: Beyond a Baptist Preacher Predator and His Gang* (Cedarburg, Wis.: Foremost, 2009).

25. Also check out these two excellent books: Diane Mandt Langberg, *Counseling Survivors of Sexual Abuse* (Maitland, Fla.: Xulon Press, 2003); Langberg, *On the Threshold of Hope: Opening the Door to Healing for Survivors of Sexual Abuse* (Wheaton, Ill.: Tyndale, 1999).

commander-in-chief, a man after God's own heart, Scripture isn't concerned about preserving his reputation.

While the text never states explicitly that David forced her to have sex, the fact that the text places all of the blame for what happened on him and none of it on her, and that the crime warranted a death sentence for him, makes a highly compelling argument that he raped her. I'd call it a power rape.

And yet shockingly, God was still able to bring good out of this tragedy. The fruit of the scandalous union between David and Bathsheba, through their second son, Solomon, was an ongoing royal lineage that culminated almost a millennium later in the birth of a son who came to redeem the sins of people, including both the perpetrators and victims of rape. And Matthew doesn't gloss over the scandal in his genealogy; he specifically mentions how David and "the wife of Uriah" were the ancestors of Jesus (Matt. 1:6).

Jesus on Lust and Adultery

The issue of rape doesn't really appear in the Gospels, but adultery comes up several times. Perhaps most famously, Jesus brings it up in the context of lust in the Sermon on the Mount.

> You have heard that it was said, "You shall not commit **_adultery_**." But I say to you that everyone who looks at a **woman** with lustful intent has already committed **_adultery_** with her in his heart.
>
> — Matthew 5:27–28

While it may seem like Jesus is undermining the seventh commandment (Exod. 20:14), he's actually intensifying it. Jesus tells us that when a person looks at another person with lust, it's like committing adultery, which means there are a lot of adulterers running around.

The scribes and the Pharisees also raise the topic of adultery in the Gospels (John 8:2–11).[26]

---

26. The story of the woman caught in adultery (John 7:53–8:11) has numerous textual

> Early in the morning he [Jesus] came again to the temple. All the people came to him, and he sat down and taught them. The scribes and the Pharisees brought a **woman** who had been caught in adultery, and placing her in the midst they said to him, "Teacher, this **woman** has been caught in the act of adultery. Now in the Law Moses commanded us to stone such **women**. So what do you say?" This they said to test him, that they might have some charge to bring against him. Jesus bent down and wrote with his finger on the ground. And as they continued to ask him, he stood up and said to them, "Let him who is without sin among you be the first to throw a stone at her." And once more he bent down and wrote on the ground. But when they heard it, they went away one by one, beginning with the older ones, and Jesus was left alone with the **woman** standing before him. Jesus stood up and said to her, "**Woman**, where are they? Has no one **condemned** you?" She said, "No one, Lord." And Jesus said, "Neither do I **condemn** you; go, and from now on sin no more."
>
> — John 8:2–11

Jesus is teaching at the temple in front of a big crowd, and he is approached by the religious leaders with a woman "caught in adultery." Hypocritically, these leaders call Jesus "Teacher" but then proceed to give the teacher a "test." (I thought teachers gave tests.) Why was it a test? If Jesus says, "Stone her," he will be in trouble with Rome, which doesn't allow the Jews to put anyone to death (John 18:31). But if he says, "Don't stone her," he will be in trouble with the Jews, who value Moses and the law (including the adultery laws discussed earlier). Hence, the trap.

As I read this story, three questions come to mind. My first question is, where is the man caught in adultery? Unless I'm missing something,

---

problems, but many commentators still think it contains an accurate narrative from the life of Jesus. See the various John commentaries, or Kenneth E. Bailey, *Jesus through Middle Eastern Eyes* (Downers Grove, Ill.: InterVarsity, 2008), 229–30.

adultery usually involves a female as well as a male. Did he escape? Was he too famous to embarrass? Did he buy them off? While it's fun to speculate, we just don't know, and we don't want to make things up. All that we know is that in this situation, the male adulterer is not present, so only the female adulterer gets dragged before Jesus and publicly accused of sexual immorality. The fact that he is not there is so outrageous you might expect someone in the crowd to ask, "Hey, where's the guy?" but apparently in Jesus' day, people were accustomed to the idea that the woman is blamed while the man gets off scot-free. Some things never change.

My second question is, how's this woman feeling? She was caught in the act, grabbed by the religious leaders (they may not have given her a chance to get properly dressed), and thrust into the center of attention before Jesus and his large audience at the temple. Was she feeling:

- *abandoned*, because she has been deserted by her "beloved" partner?
- *humiliated*, because she wasn't properly attired to be the star attraction in an adultery trial?
- *vulnerable*, because she stands before a group of religious leaders not known for compassion?
- *frightened*, because she waits to hear about her fate from men eager to stone her to death?

I think it's safe to say she was probably feeling all four of these emotions as she stood alone in front of the enormous crowd, the religious leaders, and Jesus. To make things worse, she may have been quite young, since the only law that specifically mentions stoning is Adultery Law 2, where the woman was engaged, but not yet married (Deut. 22:23–24), and engagement often happened while a woman was a teen.

My third question is, what is Jesus writing on the ground? Pastors and scholars love to speculate about what he was writing: the sins of her accusers? the names of her accusers? what he's about to say? doodling? But before we do too much speculating, remember, "Don't make things up!" We don't know because the text doesn't say. If what he was writing were important, the text would tell us. Don't base a lesson or a sermon on conjecture. What's important isn't *what* he is writing but *that* he is writing. Jesus writes on the ground for an extended period of time after their question, since they continue to repeat their question, and then he continues to write for an extended period after his answer to their test, while they slowly depart.

Jesus' writing on the ground does two things. It dampens the emotions of the "lynch mob." Mobs are notoriously chaotic and frenetic, but by writing on the ground, Jesus brings calm and order and gives the leaders and the crowd an opportunity to reflect on the situation. Jesus' writing also takes the attention off the humiliated and frightened young woman and focuses it all on himself, as people try to get a glimpse of what he is writing. He first bends down and writes; he then stands up and speaks; he then bends down and writes again. His writing, his movements, and his speech are dramatic and deliberate, shifting the crowd's attention from the woman to himself and providing them an opportunity to reflect on their own sins.

As I watched my wife teach Sunday school recently, I noticed how everyone in the class watched her write things on the whiteboard. We're curious to see what she'll write; there's a bit of drama involved. Similarly, as Jesus diverts attention from the woman and focuses it on himself by writing, he is showing compassion on this poor woman.

Before moving on, we need to look at what Jesus says about sin. First, when the young woman is alone with Jesus, he doesn't condemn her, but he also tells her not to sin anymore. Jesus takes sin seriously, and he expects his followers to do the same. Sin has serious consequences.

Second, his statement, "Let him who is without sin among you be the first to throw a stone" implies that everyone has sins; at least that's how all the leaders interpret it as they put down their stones and leave. Jesus' "answer" aced the leaders' test, not only by upholding the Mosaic law but also by exposing their hypocrisy. It's easy to condemn people guilty of sexual sins we don't struggle with (prostitution? adultery? homosexuality?), but Jesus' words here should caution against hasty condemnations, lest we become like these hypocritical religious leaders. Before we cast stones at these religious leaders "caught in the act" of hypocrisy, Jesus' words should caution us against quickly judging people we think are too judgmental. We all fall short; that's why we all need Jesus.

Fraternities, Froshbooks, and Forgiveness

A few years ago our family was vacationing in Northern California and we visited my alma mater, Stanford. During our campus tour, our guide made a curious offhand comment about her residence, so I asked her about it. When she mentioned the address, it sounded familiar. I said, "You live in my old fraternity house."

She said, "Yeah, I think they got kicked off campus." After a little research I discovered that my brothers were booted about fifteen years earlier. We probably deserved it.

I don't know everything that went on during my two years living in the fraternity, but based on what I've learned about sexual assaults on campus, it is likely that women were being raped. When I was a pledge, we were told to steal Froshbooks, booklets with pictures of all the first year students, so the members could check out the "fresh meat." Most college rapes occur when a woman is in her first or second year.

When my fraternity had parties, women could come and drink for free. There was always plenty of beer, as well as sweet drinks with some potent alcohol mixed in, like rum or Everclear. Many college rapes involve alcohol and intoxication.

During some of the longer parties, we blocked out one of the men's bathrooms and made it available for women who wanted to shower to freshen up for the evening. Unbeknownst to the female showerers, there was a hole that guys could peek through to watch the women shower.

I never stole a Froshbook, I never got a woman drunk, I never looked through the peephole, but I was aware that these things were going on and lacked the courage to stop them. I wasn't like Nathan the prophet, who risked his life to challenge his king. I deeply regret that. I wish I could ask forgiveness from the victimized women.

We know that the vast majority of rapes are committed by a small minority of men, the serial rapists. But these rapists will continue to victimize women unless those of us who suspect something is wrong don't step up and say something to stop them. If you see something suspicious at school, at home, at work, or at church, speak up. We need to be less like David's messenger accomplices and more like Nathan, God's prophet.

At the beginning of the chapter, I asked why God doesn't smite rapists. Perhaps the reason he doesn't smite them is because even rapists, just like adulterers and other sinners like me, need an opportunity to be forgiven like David.

CHAPTER 6

INCESTERS

"I'm Your Big Brother Marrying Your Mother"

In the film *Monsters University* (2013), Mike (voiced by Billy Crystal) and Sulley (voiced by John Goodman) return to their fraternity to be informed of "good news" from their fraternity brothers at Oozma Kappa, Don and Scott, regarding Don's engagement to Scott's mother, Sherri.

Don: Sherri and I are engaged.

Sulley: Who's Sherri?

Scott: She's my mom.

Sherri: If it isn't my two favorite fellows.

Scott: This is so uncomfortable.

Don: Oh, come on, Scott. I don't want you to think of me as your new dad; after all, we're fraternity brothers.

Scott: This is so weird.

Don: Think of me as your big brother that's marrying your mother ... We're brothers who share the same mom/wife.

I think we can all agree that incest feels weird (except for monsters and royals). But as we look at the issue in the world of the Old Testament, we'll need a word for someone who commits incest. *Incestuous people* is too long. *Sibling spouses* doesn't fit all the scenarios. *Monstrous marriages* could apply to many non-incestuous unions. I think *incesters* is the logical choice. At least that's what I'll call them in this chapter. We'll see if it catches on.

While the topic of incest can be humorous, as this animated dialogue shows, the reality of incest is highly disturbing, since much sexual abuse is incestuous, father to daughter, brother to sister, uncle to nephew, etc.[1] Humor is one way to cope with the troubling nature of incest. The Old Testament, however, deals with it directly just as it does with polygamy, prostitution, rape, and adultery — by legislating against it and narrating its tragic consequences.

Incest Laws: Mothers and Sisters, Aunts and Daughters

The longest section of incest laws appears in Leviticus 18:6–18, which most of you have probably already memorized, since Leviticus is such a popular book for devotions and memorization. But for the sake of the minority who have yet to hide these incest laws in their hearts, I'll discuss them now. The laws are rather repetitious, so I'll just list the first six verses, starting in Leviticus 18:6.

> None of you shall approach any one of his close relatives to <u>uncover nakedness</u>. **I am the LORD**.
>
> You shall not uncover the nakedness of your ***father***, which is the <u>nakedness</u> of your **mother**; she is your mother, you shall not uncover her nakedness.
>
> You shall not <u>uncover the nakedness</u> of your ***father's wife***; it is your father's <u>nakedness</u>.
>
> You shall not <u>uncover the nakedness</u> of your **sister**, your ***father's* daughter** or your **mother's daughter**, whether brought up in the family or in another home.
>
> You shall not <u>uncover the nakedness</u> of your son's

---

1. In this chapter, I'll focus on incest between males and females, since there aren't any clear examples of homosexual incest in Scripture.

daughter or of your **daughter's daughter**, for their naked-ness is your own nakedness.

You shall not uncover the nakedness of your *father's wife's daughter*, brought up in your *father's* family, since she is your **sister**.

—Leviticus 18:6–11

Leviticus 18 mentions ten categories of incest that are forbidden, which I've formatted in Table of Incestry 1. The text uses the language of "uncovering nakedness" as a euphemism for sexual intercourse.[2] The table lists the laws, biblical examples, and any children that resulted from the incestuous unions. Leviticus 18 addresses these laws to men, but all of these scenarios also involve women.

The first law involving "close relatives" expresses the general principle that close family members are off limits. Among the specific laws, there's a gradual progression from closer relatives (your mother, your sister) to more distant ones (your daughter-in-law, your sister-in-law). These laws don't mention any penalties for the various forms of incest.[3] Curiously, sex with a daughter is not explicitly mentioned, perhaps because it was assumed to be obviously wrong and because the restriction was already implied by the first prohibition against sex with close relatives and the other prohibition against sex with both a mother and her daughter. While there are many forbidden forms of incest, it was okay to do more than kiss your cousin, and as we see in Genesis, there are several examples of mating cousins, which seems wrong to us, but in their context, cousin marriage was preferable to marriage outside their clan.

Leviticus 20 is not as exhaustive as Leviticus 18 in its list of forbidden sexual relationships with family members; it includes only six types of prohibited incest, which I've formatted in Table of Incestry 2. While Leviticus 18 spoke in second person terms ("your mother"), Leviticus 20 generally speaks in third person terms ("his father's wife";

2. Most English translations go with the literal "uncovering nakedness" in Leviticus 18:6–18, but the NIV renders it less idiomatically as "having sexual relations."
3. Although in the broader context of the entire chapter, Yahweh declares that people who commit these sins will be cut off from their people (Lev. 18:29).

Table of Incestry 1
(Leviticus 18)

Lev. 18	Do not uncover the nakedness of . . .	Biblical Examples of This Form of Incest → Children
18:6	close relatives	all the examples below?
18:7	your mother	
18:8	your father's wife	Reuben and Bilhah (Gen. 35:22; 49:4) Absalom and David's wives (2 Sam. 12:11; 16:21–22)
18:9	your sister	Cain and his sister? (Gen. 4:17) → Enoch Seth and his sister? (Gen. 5:6) → Enosh
18:9, 11	your half sister[a] or your stepsister	Abraham and Sarah (Gen. 20:12) → Isaac Amnon and Tamar (2 Sam. 13:14)
18:10	your granddaughters[b]	
18:12–14	your aunts[c]	Nahor and niece[d] Milcah (Gen. 11:29) → Bethuel Amrah and Jochebed (Exod. 6:20) → Moses, Aaron, Miriam
18:15	your daughter-in-law	Tamar and Judah (Gen. 38:18) → Perez
18:16	your sister-in-law	Onan and Tamar (Gen. 38:8–9)
18:17	a woman and her daughter, or granddaughters	Lot & daughters (Gen. 19:30–38) → Ammon, Moab
18:18	two sisters[e]	Jacob & Leah / Rachel (Gen. 29:23–30) → 8 tribes
	but marriage to a cousin is not forbidden	Isaac & Rebekah (Gen. 24:67) → Jacob Esau & Mahalath (Gen. 28:9) Jacob & Leah / Rachel (Gen. 29:23–30) → 8 tribes Othniel & Achsah (Judg. 1:12–13)

[a] Under the category of half sister, I've combined your father's daughter and your mother's daughter.
[b] Under the category of granddaughter, I've combined your son's daughter and your daughter's daughter.
[c] Under the category of aunts, I've combined your father's sister, your mother's sister, and your father's brother's wife.
[d] Even though it isn't expressly forbidden in these laws, I include the example of uncle-niece incest between Nahor and Milcah under the category of aunt-nephew incest, which presumably is comparable.
[e] This law was also discussed in the context of polygamy laws in chapter 3.

Table of Incestry 2 (Leviticus 20)		
Lev. 20	**The man who lies with . . .**	**. . . shall be punished with . . .**
20:11	his father's wife	death
20:12	his daughter-in-law	death
20:14	both a woman & her mother	death
20:17	his sister, or half sister	being cut off
20:19–20	his aunt	childlessness
20:21	his sister-in-law	childlessness

except in 20:19). Leviticus 20 uses both the sexual euphemisms of "uncovering nakedness" and "lying with" someone.

All six of these incestuous relationships in Leviticus 20 were already mentioned in Leviticus 18, but now punishments are given: death for the first three, childlessness for the last two, and being cut off from the Israelite community for incest with sisters.

Deuteronomy includes two short sections addressing three forms of incest, each of which are already covered in Leviticus. A man is prohibited from marrying his father's wife (Deut. 22:30), and a curse is declared on anyone who lies with his father's wife, his sister, or his mother-in-law (Deut. 27:20, 22–23).

What can we learn from these laws about sex, marriage, and incest?

First, God wants to be involved in our sex lives. The first law concludes with the authoritative declaration "I am Yahweh." God is establishing these laws, and as the creator not only of all of his divine image-bearers but also of sex itself, he gives the laws authority and legitimacy.

Second, God wants sex to be between one man and one woman — unique, special, intimate, and private — and, therefore, it is not to be shared with other members of the family. Food, drink, shelter, and many other things are meant to be shared generously in a spirit of hospitality, but not sex.

Third, God wants to protect women and children from predatory members of their own families.[4] These laws are generally addressed to men, who in that culture would have been the ones typically to initiate sexual relationships, seen most obviously in the incestuous rapes committed by David's sons Amnon and Absalom. The fact that several of these forms of incest warranted the death penalty shows how seriously God wanted incest to be taken.

A Scandalous History Reveals a Merciful God

For eight of the ten forbidden cases of incest in Leviticus 18, we find an example of it in the Old Testament. Many of these I discuss elsewhere.

- Reuben had sex with his father Jacob's concubine, Bilhah, as did Absalom with his father David's concubines (see chapter 5).
- Cain and Seth seemed to have each married one of their sisters (see below).
- Abraham and Sarah were half-siblings (see chapters 3–5), as were Amnon and Tamar (see below).
- Abraham's brother Nahor married his niece Milcah, and Moses' mother, Jochebed, was the aunt of his father, Amrah.
- Tamar had sexual relations with both her brother-in-law and her father-in-law (see chapter 4).
- Lot's two daughters seduced him while drunk in order to carry on his lineage (see below).
- Jacob married two sisters, Leah and Rachel (see chapter 3).
- There are multiple examples of mating cousins, but that wasn't forbidden.

---

4. Obviously, men can sexually abuse other males, but I'll briefly address this topic in chapter 7.

We'll look at a few of these examples in more depth, but some questions should come to mind here. If so many forms of incest were forbidden by these laws, why are there so many incesters in the Old Testament? And why are so many of the key figures of the Old Testament (Abraham, Isaac, Jacob, Judah, Moses, and Aaron) associated with incest, as participants or offspring?

First, as the text is laid out, many of these incestuous encounters take place long before these laws are established.[5] Most of these examples occur in the book of Genesis, before the incest laws of Leviticus and Deuteronomy were given to Moses. It would be unreasonable to hold people to a divine standard that had yet to be established.

Second, it was preferable for Abraham's family to marry within their clan, or extended family, because of the shared values, customs, and religious practices (Gen. 24:3–4; 28:1–2; Judg. 14:3).[6] There weren't many worshipers of Yahweh during Israel's early history, so that limited marital options. Paul expresses a similar value as he tells the Christians in Corinth not to be "unequally yoked" with unbelievers (2 Cor. 6:14).

Third, except in the case of levirate marriage, the text never endorses incest. An absence of condemnation does not constitute an affirmation. All of these biblical incestuous relationships have problems. Somewhat akin to the grayness of polygamy (see chapter 3), these relationships are at best non-ideal (Sarah and Abraham) or at worse horribly evil (Amnon's rape of his half sister Tamar). Sins associated with incest include deception (Abraham), drunkenness (Lot), and rape (Amnon and Absalom).

Certain atheist websites like to point out the problem of incest in the Bible, claiming that it undermines Scripture's message, but I believe the opposite is true.[7] The fact that Israel's history includes stories of

---

5. As I've said previously, many scholars think both the laws and narratives of the Pentateuch were written much later than they are set, during the monarchy or even later, but I'm not addressing compositional dating issues here.

6. Anthropologists call marriage within a clan or tribe *endogamy*, so we can also call Abraham an endogamist.

7. On incest in the Bible, here's what a skeptic says: *http://skepticsannotatedbible.com/ says_about/incest.html.*

ancestor incest argues for its authenticity, because national histories are usually purified to make one's forefathers into heroes, and not into prostitutes, rapists, and incesters. A scandalous history reveals a merciful God. Once again we see how God works through highly flawed individuals to accomplish his purposes.

"I'm My Own Grandpa"

If you think incest is weird, wild, and bewildering, check out the song "I'm My Own Grandpa," written in 1947.[8] The song tells the story of a man who became his own grandpa when his wife's daughter married his own father. ("Now, if my wife is my grandmother, then I'm her grandchild …") So, if you want to avoid becoming your own grandpa (or grandma), don't let your dad (or mother) marry the daughter (or son) of your wife (or husband). According to Old Testament incest laws, this bizarre type of family situation would not have been prevented, but fortunately, there's no record of it happening in the Bible.

Did Cain Really Marry His Sister?

In chapter 1 I asked, "Did Cain really marry his sister?" To explain the background, for those of you who didn't pester your Sunday school teachers with this question, after Cain killed his brother Abel, the text says he "knew his wife and she conceived" (Gen. 4:17), but the text doesn't mention anyone else being around except his parents. The precocious eight-year-old will, therefore, ask this question to his or her Sunday school teacher. When your child or student asks you this question, here are three options for possible responses.

Option 1: "Yes, Cain married his sister." This is the most popular answer, backed up by the reason that there weren't any other ways to

---

8. "I'm My Own Grandpa" is written by Dwight Latham and Moe Jaffe. Personally, I prefer the version performed by Ray Stevens. These two websites include helpful graphics: *http://gean.wwco.com/grandpa/* and *https://www.youtube.com/watch?v=eYlJH81dSiw&feature=kp.*

procreate at the beginning except by sibling love. There are two big problems with Option 1. One, marrying your sister is clearly incest, a crime in Leviticus that's later punishable by death (Lev. 20:17). Two, no other sisters are mentioned in the text yet, so we have to make her up (but the text does later mention other sons and daughters of Adam in Genesis 5:4).

Option 2: "No, not his sister, his mother." While many people consider only Option 1, Option 2 is perhaps more reasonable, since Eve is the only woman mentioned so far in the text. But in the incestuous pecking order, I think sex with Mother is worse than sex with Sister. Like Option 1, this incest is also later worthy of death (Lev. 20:11). While Eve has been mentioned, the text probably wouldn't call her Cain's wife. So there are even more problems with this option.

Option 3: "No, not his sister, someone else." God must have somehow made other people the text doesn't tell us about. But isn't Eve "the mother of all living" (Gen. 3:20)? Yes, but she didn't give birth to Adam, so God could have created other people from the ground like Adam, from spare ribs like Eve, or in any number of other creative ways. The last time a man needed a spouse, God just created one, so there's a precedent already established for divine spousal provision. If there were other people around already, it would explain why Cain was worried that other people were going to kill him (Gen. 4:14).

Each of these options has problems, but I prefer Option 3 since it has the least number of problems and it explains the other difficulty of Cain's irrational fear of others. But Genesis doesn't tell us where Cain's wife came from, so we should be careful to remember, "Don't make stuff up." While the identity of Cain's wife is an interesting topic to discuss, Genesis doesn't care who she was, so we probably shouldn't either. If it mattered who Cain's wife was, Genesis would have told us.

Lot Was Seduced by His Daughters

Before Sodom was destroyed, Lot's two angelic guests urged him and his family to head to the hills (Gen. 19:17), but they delayed. However, a rainstorm of fire and brimstone tends to get one's attention, so they fled and finally arrived at their intended safe cave in the hills (but without Mom, who was permanently delayed).

> Now Lot went up out of Zoar and lived in the hills with his two **daughters**, for he was afraid to live in Zoar. So he lived in a cave with his two **daughters**. And the firstborn said to the younger, "Our **father** is old, and there is not a man on earth to come in to us after the manner of all the earth. Come, let us make our **father** drink wine, and we will lie with him, that we may preserve offspring from our **father**." So they made their **father** drink wine that night. And the firstborn went in and lay with her **father**. He did not know when she lay down or when she arose. The next day, the firstborn said to the younger, "Behold, I lay last night with my **father**. Let us make him drink wine tonight also. Then you go in and lie with him, that we may preserve offspring from our **father**." So they made their **father** drink wine that night also. And the younger arose and lay with him, and he did not know when she lay down or when she arose. Thus both the **daughters** of Lot became pregnant by their **father**. The firstborn bore a son and called his name Moab. He is the **father** of the Moabites to this day. The younger also bore a son and called his name Ben-ammi. He is the **father** of the Ammonites to this day.
>
> — Genesis 19:30–38

Sex, incest, and drunkenness — I'm surprised Hollywood hasn't made a film out of this story. The older sister has a plan to get Dad drunk, sleep with him, hopefully conceive a male heir, and then repeat the process with her younger sister. Ironically, while they were still in Sodom, Lot offered his daughters to be raped by the men of the city, but they were saved by angels (Gen. 19:8), but now no one protects Lot from rape by his own daughters.[9]

What do we do with this bizarre tale? Are the actions of Lot's daughters to be condemned or affirmed? While the heading for this section in my Bible is "The Shameful Origin of Moab and Ammon," let's be careful not to make the text say things that it doesn't, since the Bible never explicitly condemns their behavior.[10]

I don't think what they did was good, but let's start by pointing out two positive aspects of the behavior of Lot's daughters. Their goal was honorable, because they wanted to produce an heir for their father, similar to the practice of levirate marriage, which involves sex that otherwise would have been considered incestuous. Their actions were also clever and resourceful, a bit like their distant relative Tamar (Genesis 38; see chapter 4).

One could argue that God viewed their action favorably because he seemed to bless the sisters' plans where success would seem to be highly unlikely. Despite being so drunk that he had no idea what happened the next day, somehow Lot's plumbing still worked, and not only was dual conception achieved during the sororal doubleheader, but in both cases male heirs were the result, so that Lot's sons were also his grandsons (but he was not his own grandpa). In the absence of a textual comment, however, we should assume the success of Lot's daughters' plan was because of fortune, not divine intervention.

While one might appreciate their resourcefulness and their desire to fulfill the first commission ("be fruitful and multiply"), it seems that in this case, the ends do not justify the means. Here are three reasons to view the actions of these two daughters negatively. First, their

---

9. For a brief discussion of early Jewish and Christian perspectives on the incidents of incest involving Lot and Reuben, see William Loader, *Making Sense of Sex: Attitudes towards Sexuality in Early Jewish and Christian Literature* (Grand Rapids, Mich.: Eerdmans, 2013), 53–54.

10. While I love my NRSV Bible (given to me by my mother almost twenty years ago; restored and recovered by me three years ago), and I appreciate the headings, some of them are misleading, and a few are just plain wrong. Be suspicious of things editors add to your Bible; see my blog post on this topic: *http://davidtlamb .com/2011/10/26/i-hate-study-bibles/*.

father could have arranged marriages with men from the nearby town of Zoar, as he had done previously in Sodom (Gen. 19:14). Second, while not mentioned among the Old Testament laws, father-daughter incest was the most abhorrent type, and the punishment for the more distant form of incest between a father and his daughter-in-law was still death. We know Lot would not have approved of these liaisons, which is why they needed to get him drunk. Third, it's never good to get someone drunk to have sex with them. This message cannot be stated loudly or often enough, particularly on college campuses. Unlike the sex between Tamar and Judah, which was consensual, the sex between these daughters and their father was not.

However, the fact that these two young women were probably experiencing severe shock and grief after their city was destroyed and their fiancees were killed should cause us to view their desperate, but improper, actions with compassion. As we move forward in history, the descendants of Lot's two sons/grandsons, Moab (the Moabites) and Ben-Ammi (the Ammonites) frequently appear in Scripture as Israel's rivals (Num. 22–24; Judg. 3:12–30; 2 Kings 3:4–27), although there are occasional unions, such as the one between the Israelite Boaz and the Moabite Ruth (Ruth 4:13), both of whom are mentioned in Jesus' genealogy (Matt. 1:5).

Amnon Raped His Own Sister

The incest between Lot and his daughters is creepy on several levels, but it is particularly unusual as an example of rape of a man by a woman. In both our modern context and in the world of the Bible, most of the perpetrators of sexual assault are men, which is the case in the rape of David's daughter Tamar by her half brother Amnon. While the tragic consequences of the rape and murder of the Levite's concubine included a civil war in Israel (Judges 19–20), Amnon's rape of Tamar resulted in a fratricide, a rebellion, and a civil war. This story follows almost immediately after the extended story of the rape of Bathsheba by David (2 Samuel 11–12).

Now Absalom, David's son, had a beautiful **sister**, whose name was Tamar. And after a time Amnon, David's son, loved her.

— 2 Samuel 13:1

Based on a scheme from his friend Jonadab, Amnon pretends to be ill and asks his father David to send his sister Tamar to care for him. She then makes cakes and brings them to Amnon in his bedroom.

But when she brought them near him to eat, he took hold of her and said to her, "Come, lie with me, **my sister**." She answered him, "No, **my brother**, do not violate me, for such a thing is not done in Israel; do not do this outrageous thing. As for me, where could I carry my shame? And as for you, you would be as one of the outrageous fools in Israel. Now therefore, please speak to the king, for he will not withhold me from you." But he would not listen to her, and being stronger than she, he violated her and lay with her. Then Amnon _**hated**_ her with very great _**hatred**_, so that the _**hatred**_ with which he _**hated**_ her was greater than the love with which he had loved her. And Amnon said to her, "Get up! Go!" But she said to him, "No, **my brother**, for this wrong in sending me away is greater than the other that you did to me." But he would not listen to her. He called the young man who served him and said, "Put **this woman** out of my presence and bolt the door after her."

— 2 Samuel 13:11–17

Royal sons often get what they want, and Amnon was no exception. His friend Jonadab's clever scheme, with Florence Nightingale overtones, assumes that as Tamar cares for her poor sick brother, she might develop feelings for him. Or perhaps it was merely a ploy to get her into his bedroom. Either way, the seduction didn't go as Amnon had planned. The highly romantic line that didn't work for Mrs. Potiphar with Joseph, "Lie with me" (Gen. 39:7, 12), also failed with Tamar, so Amnon forced himself upon her.

How should we view the incest here? The incestuous nature of this episode is emphasized by their language to each other. He calls her "my sister" and she calls him "my brother" both before and after the rape. Despite the early patriarchal example of Abraham and Sarah, as we saw before, the law forbids sexual relations between half-siblings, although the penalty was not death but merely being "cut off" (Lev. 18:9; 20:17). Yet when Tamar says "such a thing is not done in Israel," she doesn't seem to be referring to the incest (she seems okay with marrying him later) but to forced sex outside of the king's approval. Perhaps the incest laws of Leviticus were not enforced or not thought to apply to the royal family.[11]

Tamar, like her probable namesake, Judah's daughter-in-law, was an impressive woman. Everything the text says about her is positive. She was willing to serve her sick brother by preparing and delivering home-baked cakes, a task that could have easily been performed by one of their royal servants. Despite the lack of a romantic proposal, she was willing to marry him. (As David's oldest son, Amnon would probably be his father's royal successor, which would mean she would be queen.) Even after the rape, she was still willing to be his wife. Her assessment that it would be more wrong for Amnon to kick her out post-sex than to rape her in the first place, which seems nonsensical to us, reveals that the Deuteronomy rape law (see chapter 5, the section "Rape Laws: Marrying Your Rapist?"; Deut. 22:28–29) made sense to an ancient Israelite young woman. This victimized woman did not think it was sexist to marry her rapist.[12] Perhaps most impressive about Tamar was her wisdom under fire, as she reasons with her potential rapist in the moment of passion, even speaking prophetically about her fate and that of her brother. Her words came true, as she was burdened by shame and never remarried, and his foolish behavior prompted his brother Absalom to orchestrate his death (2 Sam.

11. Anderson points out that the half-sibling incest laws of Leviticus may have been written later than Amnon's rape of Tamar, despite their presence earlier in the canon; A. A. Anderson, *2 Samuel* (Dallas: Word, 1989), 172.
12. See my discussion of Tamar's perspective on her post-rape situation in *God Behaving Badly*, 61–64.

13:20, 28–29).[13] Wise brothers listen to wise sisters, but unfortunately Amnon was foolish.

Amnon not only was a fool, but he was also a liar and a rapist. He listened to his foolish friend Jonadab instead of his wise sister Tamar. He deceived her with his manipulative plan to get her into his bedroom. He raped his own sister, whom he could have married if he were willing simply to wait. Then post-sex, he threw her out, breaking the command of Deuteronomy 22 to marry her in order to provide security for her.

But almost as troubling as Amnon's rape was the fact that, although David got angry, he did nothing to punish his son for raping his daughter. Some English translations (NRSV, NJB, and CEB) include an additional phrase explaining that David didn't punish him because he loved Amnon as his oldest son.[14] While commentators are divided about whether to include this phrase (I would include it), either way it is reasonable that David would be reluctant to punish his oldest son. Perhaps, because of his own rape of Bathsheba, he didn't feel worthy to "cast the first stone." Like David, sometimes leaders in the church today are unwilling to punish men accused by women of rape, incest, or sexual abuse. This is a tragedy that must stop.

It is difficult to know how often incestuous sexual abuse occurs, but people who study the topic estimate that before age eighteen, 20–40 percent of females and 15–20 percent of males have been sexually abused.[15] If you're a victim of abuse, or know someone who is, get help, seek out a good counselor, and check out the resources by Diane Langberg in this footnote.[16]

---

13. In addition to revenge for his sister, ambition for the throne almost certainly played a factor in Absalom's plot to kill Amnon, since Amnon was David's oldest and Absalom, as third son, was probably next in line, since Chileab (David's second son) disappears from the narrative after his birth record (2 Sam. 3:2–3).

14. This additional phrase explaining David's reluctance to punish Amnon is based on the Septuagint and a Dead Sea Scrolls fragment (4QSam[a]).

15. See Diane Mandt Langberg, *Counseling Survivors of Sexual Abuse* (Maitland, Fla.: Xulon Press, 2003), 80–81.

16. Diane Mandt Langberg, *On the Threshold of Hope: Opening the Door to Healing for Survivors of Sexual Abuse* (Wheaton, Ill.: Tyndale, 1999). To understand the dynamics

John the Baptist: Herod's Lust and Jesus' Love

While Matthew's list of Jesus' ancestors includes several incesters (Abraham, Jacob, Judah, Tamar; Matt. 1:2–3), Jesus never directly addresses the subject of incest. But Mark interrupts his version of the story of Jesus to tell us how Jesus' messenger, John the Baptist, was killed for speaking out against incest in Herod's family.

Before looking at John, we need to explain what happened immediately beforehand, as Jesus has just healed two "daughters." Jesus heals a woman with a flow of blood, and after the healing, he stops to listen to her and to comfort her by calling her "daughter"; then Jesus brings back to life the dead daughter of Jairus, a leader of the synagogue (Mark 5:21–43). Because of his ministry of healing and teaching, Jesus is becoming extraordinarily popular, which causes concern and guilt for King Herod. Mark's story then moves into a flashback explaining the fate of John.

> But when Herod heard of it [Jesus' popularity], he said, "John, whom I beheaded, has been raised." For it was Herod who had sent and seized John and bound him in prison for the sake of Herodias, <u>his brother Philip's</u> **wife**, <u>because he had married her</u>. For John had been saying to Herod, "It is not lawful for you to have your brother's **wife**." And Herodias had a grudge against him and wanted to put him to death. But she could not, for Herod feared John, knowing that he was a righteous and holy man, and he kept him safe. When he heard him, he was greatly perplexed, and yet he heard him gladly.
>
> But an opportunity came when Herod on his birthday gave a banquet for his nobles and military commanders and the leading men of Galilee. For when <u>Herodias's</u> **daughter**

---

behind abuse in the church, see Diane Langberg, "Clergy Sexual Abuse," in *Abuse, Women and the Bible*, ed. C. C. Kroeger and J. R. Beck (Grand Rapids, Mich.: Baker, 1996).

came in and danced, she pleased Herod and his guests. And
the king said to the **girl**, "Ask me for whatever you wish, and
I will give it to you." And he vowed to her, "Whatever you
ask me, I will give you, up to half of my kingdom." And she
went out and said to her **mother**, "For what should I ask?"
And she said, "The head of John the Baptist." And she came
in immediately with haste to the king and asked, saying, "I
want you to give me at once the head of John the Baptist on
a platter." And the king was exceedingly sorry, but because
of his oaths and his guests he did not want to break his word
to her. And immediately the king sent an executioner with
orders to bring John's head. He went and beheaded him in
the prison and brought his head on a platter and gave it to the
girl, and the **girl** gave it to her **mother**. When his disciples
heard of it, they came and took his body and laid it in a tomb.

— Mark 6:16–29

The Herodian family is confusing, but we can figure it out. This
story involves three Herods and a Herodias. Herod the Great was the
guy who tried to kill baby Jesus (Matt. 2:1–19), so not particularly
great; I'd call him Herod the Evil. He doesn't appear in this story, but
he had two sons named Herod, and the story centers around these two.
In this text, Herod Antipas is called simply Herod, and Herod Philip
is called Philip. To avoid confusion, I'll just call them by the names the
text does. Herod and Philip had different mothers, so they were half
brothers. Clear so far? Okay, good.

So Philip married his half niece Herodias (her grandfather Herod
the Great was Philip's father), which technically isn't forbidden by
the law but still borders on incest, since Leviticus forbade marriage
between aunts and nephews, as well as between close relatives (Lev.
18:6, 12–14). While you might think all of these Herods were Romans
since they were in power, they actually were Jewish, basically puppet
rulers Rome allowed to give Jews a sense of self-government. As Jews,
they should have been under the authority of Old Testament laws like
Leviticus.

While Herod was visiting his brother Philip in Rome, Herod and Philip's wife Herodias "fell in love." They each divorced their spouses and married each other. Thus, this couple repeats the borderline incest between half uncle and half niece perpetrated initially by Philip and Herodias, but that was nothing compared with the full-fledged incest of marrying your brother's wife while he is still living, as is prohibited in the law (Lev. 18:16; 20:21). Herod manages to achieve a level-two incest in one union, which prompted the rebuke from John the Baptist, "It is not lawful for you to have your brother's wife." Ah, but it gets worse.

Since John publicly disapproves of this marriage, Herodias hates him and wants him dead. She has an opportunity to implement her scheme during Herod's big birthday bash. Herodias has already personally benefitted from her husband's incestuous disposition, so she decides to appeal to that by sending in her daughter to dance before the crowd. She isn't named in the Gospels, but from the Jewish historian Josephus we learn her name is Salome.[17] Just to be clear about the incestuous overtones, the law forbids a man from having sex with both a mother and her daughter (Lev. 18:17; 20:14). Salome "pleased" Herod and his guests, who were probably in various stages of intoxication. While the text doesn't make it explicit, it is difficult to imagine that some serious incestuous lusting toward his stepdaughter was not going on at this royal banquet, since Herod offered to give her half his kingdom. While it's Herod's birthday, Herodias gets her wish right away; she instructs her daughter Salome to ask for John's head on a platter, and Herod reluctantly obliges. The anti-incest messenger is thus permanently silenced.

By positioning the narrative of John's death in chapter 6 after the healings of two women in chapter 5, Mark has set up a contrast between Herod's incestuous lust toward two females, his stepdaughter and his niece/sister-in-law, and Jesus' compassionate love for two females, Jairus' daughter and the "daughter" with the flow of blood. While worldly leaders may exploit or abuse women and girls, Jesus

---

17. Josephus, *Antiquities* XVIII.136.

serves and heals women and girls. Jesus, therefore, models for all of us how male leaders should treat females with honor, respect, and love.

Sexual Abuse and Incest

I've invited my wife Shannon to share her perspective on this topic to conclude, so the rest of the words you read in this chapter are hers.

Dave and I were walking the dog while talking about the next chapter in his book (not an uncommon activity). The topic was incest, and we were laughing about the cleverness of "I'm My Own Grandpa" and the peculiarity of some of the Levitical laws. When I turned to Dave and said, "You know, some of your good friends are victims of incest," he stopped in his tracks.

Victims of sexual abuse don't talk about it much. Besides being an intensely personal and uncomfortable subject, many of us have harbored feelings that the abuse was somehow our fault, which is exacerbated if we were children and were abused by adults. (When I was six, I was abused by a babysitter.) After all, the adult knows what's right and wrong, right?

But it's worse for victims of incest. What if the abuse came at the hands of your uncle or your father? Who could you tell? Telling would vilify a person you love — or feel you should love — someone who appears to everyone else to be a wonderful, even godly, person. Who would believe you, a child? When the mother of a friend of mine finally believed her and told the elders of the church, the leadership chose to believe their fellow elder rather than the preteen girl who seemed to be a bit troubled.

Healing for both the victim and the perpetrator can come only when evil is brought to light. But bringing incest to light takes great courage. It requires hope that there can be healing.

A number of years ago I was on the prayer team for a large Christian conference. Before the students arrived, the person guiding us asked us to listen to God for words, images, and Scripture that would bless the people we would pray for. I listened. I heard nothing, which was a bit troubling. To make matters worse, my breasts got uncomfortably hot. And the more I prayed, the hotter they got. Talk about awkward. I wasn't sure what was happening. Was I sick? What was I going to say when someone asked me for prayer? "Hi, I'm Shannon, and I've got burning boobs"?! But the meeting started, and those of us on the prayer team lined the walls of the room to be accessible for those who wanted prayer.

A young woman threw herself into my arms and started weeping. She didn't tell me why. After her sobs stopped, I told her (feeling more than a bit self-conscious) about my experience earlier that evening. She pulled away and looked at me with a shocked expression. For the past couple of months, her father had been creeping into her room late at night to fondle her breasts. She didn't feel she could tell anyone; she had actually promised him she wouldn't tell. She felt unclean, and she was terrified he would soon want to do more. She had no idea what to do. But God spoke to her through my unique physical manifestation. God knew her situation, and now she could get help. It was a light shining into her darkness. She wasn't alone. Jesus would rescue her. After prayer I was able to refer her to a counselor, who helped her make a plan for returning home.

I love the stories of Jairus and the bleeding woman in Mark 5 that Dave mentioned earlier. Jairus' daughter has an amazing dad. He risks everything, his reputation and career, to get help for her. The woman has no one to look out for her. She is impoverished, outcast, and utterly alone. When Jesus steps into her life, he acts like her dad, even calling her "daughter." She is important to him, important enough to reschedule a critical meeting. And Jesus offers her not only healing but dignity: "Your faith has healed you. Go in peace" (Mark 5:34 NIV).

Jesus' words here are a message of hope our friends who have suffered from incest need to hear. Your earthly father, uncle, or brother may not have cared for you at his own expense. He may not have protected you. He even may have abused you. But Jesus sees you and your struggle. Jesus will stop in the midst of the crowd for you. He will go to great, even awkward, lengths to tell you how much he loves you. Jesus can be your rescuer. You are not alone.

CHAPTER 7

HOMOSEXUALS AND SODOMITES

"Why Didn't You Talk about Homosexuality?"

"Why didn't you talk about homosexuality?" My friend Jesse asked me this question when he saw the topics included in *God Behaving Badly*. He was quite concerned. "Were you afraid? It's only the most controversial topic in the world right now. What are you, chicken?" Fortunately, he didn't totally shame me (and himself) by resorting to the *Arrested Development* chicken dance.[1]

Jesse is not alone. Several bloggers also said my avoidance of the controversial topic of homosexuality was the biggest drawback of the book.[2] I see their point. I agree that the issue of homosexuality is one of the most controversial in our culture now. I agree that, while

---

1. The "chicken dance" was initially made famous by Gob on the TV show *Arrested Development*, first appearing in "Staff Infection," the fifteenth episode of season one.
2. For example, see reviews by Jamie Duguid (*http://www.wtsbooks.com/god-behaving-badly-david-lamb-9780830838264*; under WTS Reviews), and Tim Ghali (*http://www.blackcoffeereflections.com/2011/12/06/review-of-god-behaving-badly-by-dave-lamb/*).

some Christians are talking about it, many avoid the subject, perhaps because of fear. I agree that Christians need to address the topic boldly and biblically.

However, my response to Jesse and my blogging friends, as well as my friends in the LGBT[3] community, is this: I didn't talk about homosexuality in *God Behaving Badly* because the Old Testament, my focus for the book, is not particularly concerned about homosexuality. Guess how many times the words *homosexual* or *homosexuality* appear in the Old Testament. Zero for both. I checked numerous English translations (KJV, NKJV, ESV, NASB, NRSV, NIV, RSV, NJB). The words are just not there. None of the words from the acronym LGBT are there either. (But the KJV does speak of "gay" clothes in James 2:3.) As we've seen in the previous chapters, we find plenty of examples of behavior perceived to be sexually scandalous — including prostitution, polygamy, rape, adultery, and incest — in the pages of the Old Testament, but there are no examples of homosexual acts.[4] Homosexuality is controversial in our culture, but not in the pages of the Old Testament.

More Concerned about Goat-Boiling Than Homosexuality

While words related to homosexuality never appear in the Old Testament, the issue is addressed briefly in two verses in Leviticus.

> You shall not lie with a male as with a woman; it is an abomination.
>
> — Leviticus 18:22

---

3. LGBT stands for "Lesbian, Gay, Bisexual, and Transgender." The acronym has evolved and will probably continue to do so.

4. None of the three examples that are sometimes mentioned clearly involve homosexual activity. Ham probably didn't commit incest with Noah (Gen. 9:22; see Gordon J. Wenham, *Genesis 1–15* [Waco, Tex.: Word, 1987], 200). Jonathan "loved" David, but so did Saul, Hiram, and all of Israel and Judah, so to assume anything sexual took place between the two is a stretch (1 Sam. 16:21; 18:1, 3, 16, 20, 28; 20:17; 1 Kings 5:1). Sodom will be discussed later in this chapter.

> If a man lies with a male as with a woman, both of them
> have committed an abomination; they shall surely be put to
> death.
>
> — Leviticus 20:13

Just as it did in the laws about adultery, rape, and incest, the idiom in these two laws "to lie with" implies sex. We should first note that Leviticus clearly teaches that homosexual practice is wrong.[5] In both verses the act of a man having sex with another man is condemned, and the second law mandates the death penalty. While the severity of this punishment suggests that it's a serious sin, many other crimes warranted the same punishment, including sexual sins such as rape, adultery, and incest, as well as other sins including breaking the Sabbath, being disrespectful toward parents, and not caring for widows, orphans, and foreigners (Exod. 22:21–24; 31:14; Lev. 20:9, 11–14; Deut. 22:22, 25). There have been many times I didn't respect my parents, honor the Sabbath, or care for the marginalized as I should. According to these Old Testament laws, I — and perhaps you too — deserve death, and yet God extends grace.

Some Christians believe that these laws from Leviticus no longer apply, like the ceremonial dietary laws, which New Testament texts teach are no longer valid (Mark 7:19; Acts 10:9–16). However, there is nothing in the context of these Leviticus laws to suggest they were temporary laws meant to apply only to Israel or that it would have been fine in the context of a committed homosexual relationship. Leviticus 18 and 20 focus on general laws regarding sexual activity and idolatry, behaviors that the Canaanites and the other previous residents of the land were also condemned for. In the previous chapters, we've discussed some of these sexual prohibitions from these sections of Leviticus (incest, adultery, polygamy, etc.). Additionally, the

---

5. A book presenting a biblical argument for same-sex relationships by Matthew Vines came out unfortunately too late for me to review and include in this chapter, but from what I can gather he argues that the idea of same-sex orientation didn't exist in the ancient world (I agree), and that the Bible can be used to support same-sex marriage (I don't agree). See Matthew Vines, *God and the Gay Christian: The Biblical Case in Support of Same-Sex Relationships* (Colorado Springs: Convergent, 2014).

relevant New Testament passages share Leviticus' negative perspective on homosexual actions (Rom. 1:21–27; 1 Cor. 6:9–10; 1 Tim. 1:10).

However, despite some Christians' preoccupation with the topic, homosexuality is not a major biblical issue. The Ten Commandments are focused on the big sins (idolatry, murder, adultery, and coveting), and homosexuality isn't one of them. Leviticus doesn't even mention lesbian behavior or sexual orientation. Only a few verses in the Old Testament and New Testament mention homosexual behavior. Among Old Testament laws, in contrast to the two verses on homosexuality, there are ten verses on adultery/rape and twenty on incest (see chapters 5 and 6). In three different legal contexts, the Israelites are commanded not to boil a young goat in its mother's milk (Exod. 23:19; 34:26; Deut. 14:21). The Old Testament is much more concerned about adultery, rape, incest, and even more concerned about goat-boiling, than homosexuality. I'm sorry to disappoint you, but I'm not going to cover the "hot" topic of boiling goats in their mother's milk. (I'm sure many will say that's the biggest drawback of the book.)

This entire chapter could be devoted to this topic (homosexuality, not goat-boiling), but since the Old Testament doesn't have much to say about it other than these two laws we've just looked at, I'll direct interested readers to recent books that address the topic of homosexuality from a Christian perspective in this footnote.[6] However, the Old Testament does talk a lot about Sodom, so much of the rest of this chapter will focus on the story of Sodom, but since homosexual behavior and the city of Sodom have traditionally been linked, we will revisit the topic of homosexuality at several points along the way.

---

6. See James V. Brownson, *Bible, Gender, Sexuality: Reframing the Church's Debate on Same-Sex Relationships* (Grand Rapids, Mich.: Eerdmans, 2013); Wesley Hill, *Washed and Waiting: Reflections on Christian Faithfulness and Homosexuality* (Grand Rapids, Mich.: Zondervan, 2010); Mark Yarhouse, *Homosexuality and the Christian: A Guide for Parents, Pastors, and Friends* (Bloomington, Minn.: Bethany, 2010); Andrew Marin, *Love Is an Orientation: Elevating the Conversation with the Gay Community* (Downers Grove, Ill.: InterVarsity, 2009).

Prostitutes, Widows, and Sodomites

In contrast to a lack of concern for the topic of homosexuality, the Old Testament is preoccupied with a concern for the poor.[7] In the Old Testament, the word *poor* is mentioned 141 times (ESV), and the word *needy* appears another fifty times (ESV). The Bible has a lot to say about poverty, usually in contexts of how God shows, or how his people should show, compassion toward the poor (e.g., Exod. 22:25; Lev. 19:10; Deut. 15:7; Isa. 3:14). We'll come back to the poor later in this chapter, but the Old Testament is also more interested in other types of people that are mentioned in this book, specifically prostitutes (e.g., Tamar and Rahab) and widows (e.g., Tamar and Ruth). In the Old Testament, the word *prostitute* appears forty-four times (NIV) and *widow*, forty times (NIV). I realize that to determine how important something is biblically, you need to do more than simply compare the number of word occurrences (the word *trinity* never appears in English translations of the Bible), but these numbers still communicate a lot about who the Bible wants to talk about. The Old Testament is more interested in the poor, widows, and prostitutes (and even goat-boilers) than homosexuals.

The Old Testament is, however, concerned about Sodomites.[8] When I speak of Sodomites (note the capitalization), I am merely referring to the residents of the ancient city and not to people's sexual preferences and practices. I'll explain why in the following sections. We know the Bible is concerned about Sodomites because the word *Sodom* is mentioned thirty-nine times in the Old Testament (ESV), so almost as often as the words *prostitute* and *widow* (but not nearly as often as the poor and needy). The book of Genesis tells the story of Sodom, and just over half of these Sodom occurrences appear in Genesis (twenty), with the rest scattered throughout the rest of the Old Testament (nineteen).

---

7. I realize that speaking of "the poor" may no longer be politically correct, but I will continue to use the term since it is the one used most frequently in the Bible for those in poverty.

8. However, many English translations never include the word *Sodomites* (e.g., ESV, NIV, CEB).

The New Testament mentions the city nine more times. It's shocking that a city that was destroyed at the beginning of the Bible, during the life of Abraham, is mentioned repeatedly throughout the rest of the Bible. Despite all that fire and brimstone, the city just doesn't go away. There's a reason Sodom keeps getting mentioned. In Scripture, Sodom is used as a warning. Sodom symbolizes something, but perhaps not what you think it does.

Sodom, Sodomy, and Sodomites

We'll look at Genesis and the other Old Testament references soon, but we need to first debunk two popular perceptions of Sodom. Most people "know" two things about the city of Sodom. First, the residents committed homosexual acts, which have become so strongly associated with the city that *sodomy* is defined as "anal intercourse between men," and *sodomites* (small *s*) are "people who practice sodomy." While these terms now feel antiquated and are generally considered offensive, the connection between the city of Sodom and homosexual behavior persists.

Second, the city was destroyed by God with fire and sulfur because they were guilty of sodomy (Gen. 19:24–25). Because of Sodom's divine destruction, many Christians assume that homosexual behavior is one of the worst sins in the Bible, despite the lack of biblical references to the practice. Westboro Baptist Church (WBC) of Topeka, Kansas, advertises their website, "GOD-HATES-FAGS.COM," on the T-shirts of little girls. (How cute!) Where does WBC's anti-gay attitude come from? Not surprisingly, the story of Sodom in Genesis 19 features prominently on WBC's website. From what the rest of Scripture says, I think it's safe to say that God hates "God-hates-fags" websites. (But the big question is, does God hate goat-boilers?)

The problem with these two bits of knowledge about Sodom is that they are both wrong. Ironically, the Bible never records the Sodomites' committing sodomy, and Sodom was not destroyed for the sin of sodomy. If you don't believe me, we'll just have to see what the Bible says.

In fact, as we read the story of Sodom, what is shocking is how the text emphasizes not the divine destruction but the divine compassion. God loved the Sodomites. Perhaps we should create a website, GOD-LOVES-SODOM.COM?

Why No Judgment?

Love for Sodom? The city destroyed by fire and brimstone? That doesn't make any sense. Perhaps not yet, but hopefully it will after we read the whole story, and it begins much earlier than Genesis 19. The city of Sodom is initially introduced, rather negatively, when Abraham's nephew Lot chooses to make it his home.

> Abram settled in the land of Canaan, while Lot settled among the cities of the valley and moved his tent as far as **Sodom**. Now the men of **Sodom** were *wicked, great sinners* against the **Lord**.
>
> — Genesis 13:12–13

We learn that the people of Sodom, a long time before the city's destruction, "were wicked, great sinners against Yahweh" (Gen. 13:13), which might seem to support the perspective of WBC.[9] To be clear, this isn't a Ron Weasley type of "wicked" good, but "wicked" evil.[10] The text, however, provides no clues yet as to the nature of Sodom's sins. The only information we learn from the context is that the area surrounding Sodom was fertile, which was why Abraham's nephew Lot chose to settle there with his family and his livestock.

The last place in the text that people were described similarly was during the time of Noah, when human wickedness was also great

---

9. The text of Genesis doesn't provide precise dates, but as the text is laid out, the first description of Sodom as wicked occurs soon after Abraham arrives in the land of Canaan, when he is seventy-five years old, and its destruction happens several decades later, when Abraham is ninety-nine.

10. Ron Weasley is the best friend of the main character in the *Harry Potter* books and films. In *Harry Potter and the Sorcerer's Stone* (2001), after he sees Harry's forehead scar, he exclaims, "Wicked!"

(Gen. 6:5). God initially responded with regret over making the violence-prone humans, but then he decided to wipe them out with a flood, as you may have heard back in nursery school, saving only an ark-load of animals and Noah's family (Gen. 6:6–7).

When we find out that the people of Sodom were wicked sinners like the people of Noah's day, attentive readers (like you) should expect a Noahesque judgment to instantly befall the city. God promised that he wouldn't destroy with a flood again (Gen. 9:11), but that still left him many other options in his divine repertoire of smiting,[11] so-called acts of God such as earthquakes, wind, fire, water, snakes, lions, and she-bears (Exod. 9:23; 14:28; Num. 16:32; 21:6; 26:10; 1 Kings 13:24; 19:11–12; 2 Kings 2:24; Job 1:19). In light of the horrific judgment against humans during Noah's day, the absence of judgment against Sodom at this point is striking. Why no judgment? Here's a hint: it has something to do with divine patience.

Deliverance: God Loved the Sodomites

We don't have to wait long to hear more about Sodom, as the next chapter of Genesis narrates the first battle of the Bible, and several cities, including Sodom, are involved (Genesis 14). The story is a bit confusing, with numerous unfamiliar names of kings and cities, but basically it involves an alliance of five cities (Sodom, Gomorrah, Admah, Zeboiim, and Bela) pitted against an alliance of four cities (Elam, Goiim, Shinar, and Ellasar). The text calls the rulers of these cities "kings," but their domains weren't very large, so they were more like tribal chieftains or, in modern parlance, mayors. After being subjugated for twelve years by the four-city alliance led by Chedorlaomer of Elam, the five-city alliance, led by King Bera of Sodom, rebels. The rebellion of the five-city alliance is quashed, and many of their people and their possessions are captured by the four-city alliance. Right as you are asking, "Why is this story in the Bible?" the text informs you that Lot, nephew of Abraham, is among the captives (Gen. 14:12). There is a Lot of booty.[12]

---

11. I discuss the subject of God as smiter in *God Behaving Badly*, chapter 2.

12. My sons wanted to go on record that they didn't approve of this pun.

When Abraham discovers that Lot has been plundered, he organizes a posse to pursue the fleeing forces. Abraham and his men defeat the forces of the four-city alliance and bring back all the captured people and plunder.

> After his return from the defeat of Chedorlaomer and the kings who were with him, the king of **Sodom** went out to meet him at the Valley of Shaveh (that is, the King's Valley). And Melchizedek king of Salem brought out bread and wine. (He was priest of God Most High.) And he blessed him and said, "Blessed be Abram by God Most High, Possessor of heaven and earth; and blessed be God Most High, who has delivered your enemies into your hand!" And Abram gave him a tenth of everything. And the king of Sodom said to Abram, "Give me the persons, but take the goods for yourself." But Abram said to the king of **Sodom**, "I have lifted my hand to the LORD, God Most High, Possessor of heaven and earth, that I would not take a thread or a sandal strap or anything that is yours, lest you should say, 'I have made Abram rich.' I will take nothing but what the young men have eaten, and the share of the men who went with me. Let Aner, Eshcol, and Mamre take their share."
>
> — Genesis 14:17–24

After their victory, Abraham celebrates with the king of Sodom and with the mysterious Melchizedek, king and priest of Salem. While sharing food and drink, both Melchizedek and Abraham give credit for the triumph to God. Thus, instead of punishing the wicked city of Sodom, the first thing that God does is to deliver them in battle. The results of God's deliverance involved not only a military victory but also a freedom from oppression, since enslavement would have been the expected consequence of being captured in battle.

Why does God rescue the evil Sodomites? The text doesn't say, although the motivation for Abraham was clearly to save his nephew Lot (Gen. 14:14). But Lot wasn't the only person Abraham was concerned about. After the victory, Abraham doesn't just rescue Lot, but he brings back all the possessions of Sodom, the women, the children, and the men. Abraham also tells the king of Sodom that he doesn't want to keep anything that belongs to the Sodomites.

We shouldn't be surprised that Abraham was concerned for people outside his own family. When God promised to bless Abraham during his call, he made it clear that the divine blessing included "all the families of the earth" (Gen. 12:3), which would, therefore, include the city of Sodom. It makes sense that God would show mercy to Sodom since they were already being oppressed by the four-nation alliance. As we see in the story of Exodus, God is in the business of delivering people from oppression. However, when Sodom later shifts from victim to oppressor, God's value for deliverance from oppression leads him to destroy the city. But before cursing them in Genesis 19, God blessed Sodom through Abraham in Genesis 14. God loved the Sodomites.

Intercession: Abraham Loved the Sodomites

The city of Sodom reappears a few chapters later in Genesis. After the stories of Abraham and Hagar (Genesis 16), and Abraham and his amputated foreskin (Genesis 17), the patriarch hosts a dinner for three "men" who turn out to be Yahweh and two undercover angels (Gen. 18:1–15). Abraham's feast includes both milk and a calf, but presumably no goat-boiling. After a long meal together, Yahweh declares it's time to send his men out for some reconnaissance of Sodom, to see whether things are really as bad as he's hearing. Why does an omniscient God need to do reconnaissance? I don't know, but it seems Yahweh is reluctant to destroy them, just as he was during the time of Noah (Gen. 6:6–7), so he is going to make sure.

Abraham, being a clever patriarch, already knows what Yahweh's private investigators will discover. Sodom deserves destruction. He decides to negotiate with God, bargaining over the minimum number of righteous residents necessary to save the city (Gen. 18:23–32). Over the course of these ten verses, Abraham boldly asks Yahweh ten questions. Abraham starts at fifty righteous residents, then drops to forty-five, forty, thirty, twenty, and finally ten. (He should have kept going.) The two negotiators finally settle on a number. Yahweh tells Abraham if he finds ten righteous people, he won't destroy Sodom. This human-divine negotiation is unique in all of Scripture. Can you imagine what it would be like to interact with God like this?

I want to focus on the end of their bargaining dialogue. At the level of both thirty and ten righteous residents, Abraham pleads with Yahweh not to get angry.

> Then he said, "**Oh let not the Lord be angry**, and I will speak. Suppose *thirty* are found there." He answered, "I will not do it, if I find *thirty* there." He said, "Behold, I have undertaken to speak to the Lord. Suppose *twenty* are found there." He answered, "For the sake of *twenty* I will not destroy it." Then he said, "**Oh let not the Lord be angry**, and I will speak again but this once. Suppose *ten* are found there." He answered, "For the sake of *ten* I will not destroy it." And the LORD went his way, when he had finished speaking to Abraham, and Abraham returned to his place.
>
> — Genesis 18:30–33

Abraham is worried that his persistent badgering will cause Yahweh to erupt with anger, and as we know from the story of Uzzah and the ark (2 Sam. 6:1–8; see also *God Behaving Badly*, 27–33), when God gets mad, people die. Abraham thus perceives that by interceding for the city of Sodom, he is risking his life.

Why did Abraham care about Sodom? We assume that Lot's presence in Sodom was a factor, but the text doesn't make that clear, and Lot is never mentioned in the dialogue. However, Sodom is referred to fourteen times in Genesis 18:16–33 ("Sodom," "the city," "the whole place," "there," "it"). The text here ignores Lot and emphasizes Sodom. If Abraham were only focused on Lot, he could have just asked Yahweh to somehow rescue his nephew, which is exactly what Yahweh did later anyway. Instead, Abraham intercedes for the sake of the entire city. He is not concerned only about Lot.

Perhaps Abraham feels responsible for the city, since he had delivered them in battle once before. In any case, Abraham cares about Sodom, and he doesn't want it to be destroyed. He is willing to intercede for it boldly, even if his actions might incur divine wrath. This intercession is the second time Abraham risks his life for the residents of Sodom. So far in this book, we've looked at Abraham the polygamist, the pimp, and the incester, but now we encounter a more positive perspective on the patriarch as one who fought and interceded for a wicked city. Abraham loved the Sodomites.

When I teach this passage, I ask students, "Are Christians today generally perceived to be like Abraham, interceding on the behalf of and risking their lives for the sake of people associated with the sins of Sodom?" The unanimous answer: "No."

Christians are known more often as the ones who "hate fags." The popular perception that the church is homophobic can't be simply blamed on extremists like the folks from WBC. It's a bigger problem than that. Many people outside the church, particularly younger folks, consider Christians to be not just anti-homosexual but also bigoted and insulting in how they speak about gays and lesbians.[13] This perception should not characterize a community that follows Jesus. In previous chapters, we've seen that Jesus shows respect and compassion for people associated with sexual problems: the Samaritan polygamist at the well, the loving prostitute, and the woman caught in adultery. And way before Jesus, Abraham understood the compassion of God. While he had his own sexual issues with polygamy and incest, Abraham still risked his life and interceded for the wicked city of Sodom.

13. See David Kinnaman and Gabe Lyons, *Unchristian: What a New Generation Really Thinks about Christianity ... and Why It Matters* (Grand Rapids, Mich.: Baker, 2007), 91–109.

Hospitality: Getting to Know You

Meanwhile, Yahweh's two investigators, whom the text now calls angels, arrive in the town of Sodom, planning to camp out in the town square overnight.

> The two angels came to **Sodom** in the evening, and Lot was sitting in the gate of **Sodom**. When Lot saw them, he rose to meet them and bowed himself with his face to the earth and said, "My lords, please turn aside to your servant's house and spend the night and wash your feet. Then you may rise up early and go on your way." They said, "No; we will spend the night in the town square." But he pressed them strongly; so they turned aside to him and entered his house. And he made them a feast and baked unleavened bread, and they ate.
>
> — Genesis 19:1–3

Lot, who has been loitering at the town gate, intercepts the two angels and first invites, then pleads, and finally commands them to stay inside at his house. At this point, one wonders, what's so bad about camping out in Sodom? We find out after dinner.

All the men of the city surround Lot's house and, being good hosts, they want to get "to know" (in the biblical sense) Lot's two visitors.[14] So they extend an invitation to the angels to be the special guests for ... a gang rape.

> But before they lay down, the men of the city, the men of **Sodom**, both *young and old, all the people to the last man*, surrounded the house. And they called to Lot, "Where are the men who came to you tonight? Bring them out to us, that we may know them." Lot went out to the men at the entrance, shut the door after him, and said, "I beg you, my brothers,

---

14. Derek Kidner, *Genesis* (Downers Grove, Ill.: InterVarsity, 1967), 136–37, persuasively argues that the verb used for "know" (*yāda'*) in Genesis 19:5 does have sexual connotations, despite the views of a few scholars who believe otherwise.

do not act so wickedly. Behold, I have two daughters who have not known any man. Let me bring them out to you, and do to them as you please. Only do nothing to these men, for they have come under the shelter of my roof." But they said, "Stand back!" And they said, "This fellow came to sojourn, and he has become the judge! Now we will deal worse with you than with them." Then they pressed hard against the man Lot, and drew near to break the door down. But the men reached out their hands and brought Lot into the house with them and shut the door. And they struck with blindness the men who were at the entrance of the house, both small and great, so that they wore themselves out groping for the door.

—Genesis 19:4–11

The extensiveness of the mob is emphasized three ways in the text: (1) "young and old," (2) "all the people," (3) "to the last man." Why the redundancy? The text wants to make it clear every man of Sodom was there. In other words, there were not ten righteous in Sodom.[15] The city is headed for divine destruction.

While it was good that Lot was unwilling to toss out his visitors to the mob, his suggestion was a horrible alternative. Instead of his guests, he offers his virgin daughters to the crowd at his door.[16] Fortunately, the angelic investigators also think Lot's idea is a bad one, so when the mob threatens to break down the door, these two strike the men outside with blindness to make them helpless. In the History Channel's miniseries *The Bible* (2013), Lot's two angelic guests were warriors with martial arts moves. I presume the ninja interpretation of the producers (Roma Downey, *Touched by an Angel*, and Mark Burnett, *Survivor*) was based on this incident—creative, but a bit of a stretch. For the residents of Sodom, being touched by an angel involved blindness, but it made the daughters of Lot into survivors.

---

15. The text here ignores the issue of whether there were any righteous women in Sodom.
16. I discuss this incident in the context of sexism in the Old Testament in *God Behaving Badly*, 60–61, and in the context of the gang rape of the Levite's concubine in chapter 5 in this book.

Another factor often overlooked when Sodom is discussed is the numerous warnings given by the two angels that were ignored by the residents of the city. The angelic touch of blindness should have gotten the attention of all the Sodomites. The angels also tell Lot to let the other residents of the city know what is coming, both family and friends, and that they should flee. The angels twice say to include "anyone" in their message to escape (Gen. 19:12). In the spirit of Jesus' command to turn the other cheek (Matt. 5:39), God's messengers want the people who just attempted to gang rape them to be warned, so they will have a chance to get out. Tragically, Lot warns only his daughters' fiancees, and they think he's just joking. When Lot and his family don't do anything, the angels drag them out of town to save them, but many more could have been spared if warnings were circulated and heeded. A warning is an act of love, so this angelic message was yet another way God was trying to love Sodom. Unfortunately, the Sodomites choose to ignore multiple warnings from God and his messengers.

Apparently, the attempted gang rape of traveling foreigners by the entire city provided Yahweh's two investigators with enough information about the city to render a guilty verdict. It needed to be destroyed. In yet another of many parallels to Noah and the flood story, Lot and his family are saved from the coming judgment when the angels rush them out of town before fire and brimstone rain down from heaven (Gen. 19:15–25).

Divine judgment did finally come to Sodom, but beforehand, God was slow to anger and showed compassion on the city. We discover Sodom is wicked in Genesis 13, but God and Abraham show mercy by delivering them from captivity and oppression in Genesis 14. God is willing to negotiate with Abraham, who risks his life for Sodom, in Genesis 18. God wants to double-check before destroying Sodom in Genesis 19. The angels give numerous warnings to the Sodomites, all of which are ignored. God does not destroy all the residents of Sodom; he forces Lot, Lot's wife, and Lot's daughters to flee despite their reluctance to leave. God loved Sodom, but he also eventually judged Sodom.

The destruction of Sodom is told in only two verses (Gen. 19:24–25), and unfortunately that's the only part of the story that gets remembered, but that's not what the text emphasizes in the story of Sodom beginning back in Genesis 13. As we examine the whole story of the Sodomites, we see divine destruction came about only after divine deliverance, divine compassion, divine negotiation, divine reconnaissance, divine patience, and divine warning.

The Sins of Sodom: Inhospitality and Injustice

For God to wipe out an entire city, its residents must have done something truly heinous. So what was the sin of Sodom? The answer may seem obvious, but the text is actually not clear. While Sodom will be forever associated with homosexual behavior because the men of Sodom wanted to have sex with the two angels, they never succeed in their quest. It is reasonable to assume that they were successful in the past at performing similar deeds, but one needs to read the text of Genesis 19 carefully before coming to definitive conclusions about the nature of their wickedness. Don't make stuff up. The Sodomites do not actually have sex with Yahweh's angels or Lot's daughters in the biblical story. The text never records them performing a homosexual act, but it does record other crimes they do commit.[17]

The fact that they were attempting a gang rape does make the nature of their sexual crime seem more severe, and yet once again the text merely records their intention, not their performance of this deed. At this point we need to observe that it was only because of Yahweh's intervention at the hands of his angelic investigators that Lot's daughters were spared the fate that their foolish father proposed. God once again delivered a victim from a horrible situation.[18]

The text of Genesis 19 does, however, record two sins that were

---

17. The view that Sodom was primarily guilty of homosexual behavior finds some support in Jude 7, which speaks of "sexual immorality" and "unnatural desire"; however, the exact nature of Sodom's sin isn't clear from this verse, and other sins receive more biblical support.
18. Tragically, the Levite's concubine was not spared by divine intervention in a strikingly similar situation (Judg. 19:22–30; see chapter 5).

committed by Sodom: inhospitality and injustice. First, their mistreatment and verbal abuse of these two foreign visitors constitutes a severe lack of hospitality. And their inhospitality was not just intended; it was actualized. Since foreigners are in a position of weakness, they are easily exploited, as the Sodomites attempted to do. For this reason, in the law, God repeatedly tells his people to care for strangers (Exod. 22:21; 23:9; Lev. 19:10; Deut. 10:19; 24:17). The theme of welcoming strangers is emphasized in several ways in the context of Genesis 18–19, as first Abraham lavishly caters to the needs of Yahweh and the two angels (Gen. 18:1–8) and then Lot tenaciously pursues the angels, protects them, and provides for them, even offering his daughters in their place. In case you doubt that hospitality is the primary issue here, Jesus also connects the sin of Sodom directly to inhospitality when he states that the cities that do not welcome his disciples will be treated worse than Sodom (Matt. 10:13–15; see also 11:20–24; more on this soon).

While Sodom was clearly guilty of inhospitality, the text also emphasizes that they were condemned because of injustice. Yahweh tells Abraham that the outcry against Sodom was great (Gen. 18:20–21).

> Then the LORD said, "Because the *outcry* against Sodom and Gomorrah is **great** and their sin is very grave, I will go down to see whether they have done altogether according to the *outcry* that has come to me. And if not, I will know."
> — Genesis 18:20–21

Later the angels say essentially the same thing when they tell Lot why Yahweh is going to destroy the city.

> Then the men said to Lot, "Have you **anyone** else here? Sons-in-law, sons, daughters, or **anyone** you have in the city, bring them out of the place. For we are about to destroy this place, because the *outcry* against its people has become **great** before the LORD, and the LORD has sent us to destroy it."
> — Genesis 19:12–13

The residents of Sodom were condemned because they were oppressing people. Sodom's victims cried out to God, he heard them, and he decided to deliver them, because that's what God does. While we don't know exactly what form of injustice prompted their great cries for help, it may have involved gang rapes and a lack of hospitality toward foreigners.

The word for "outcry" used to describe the plea for help from Sodom's victims (Gen. 18:20–21; 19:13) is the same word used when Israel "cried" to Yahweh during their enslavement and oppression in Egypt (Exod. 2:23; 3:7, 9).[19] Just as Yahweh would show mercy toward Abraham's descendants in Exodus, he would show mercy to the victims of Abraham's neighbors in Genesis. People who teach about the sins of Sodom but ignore the sins of inhospitality and injustice in the story are not taking the text seriously.

I'm a Sodomite

I realize that some of you may not be convinced that Sodom's sins primarily involved a lack of hospitality and justice, so let's look at some of the other biblical texts that mention Sodom. In many other passages in the Old Testament, Sodom serves as a general warning about imminent judgment (Deut. 29:23; Isa. 3:9; 13:19; Jer. 49:18; Zeph. 2:9). The prophet Isaiah speaks to the Judean leaders and calls them "rulers of Sodom" (Isa. 1:10) and then details how they need to repent of their unjust ways: "do good; seek justice, rescue the oppressed, defend the orphan, plead for the widow" (Isa. 1:17 NRSV). Isaiah clearly links Sodom to injustice.

But outside of Genesis 19, the clearest expression of what Sodom's sin entailed appears in the context of Ezekiel's harsh condemnation of Judah as a faithless bride and a sister of Sodom.

> As I live, declares the Lord God, your sister **Sodom** and her daughters have not done as you and your daughters have done. Behold, this was the guilt of your sister **Sodom**: she and her daughters had <u>pride, excess of food, and prosperous</u>

---

19. There are two slightly different spellings for the same Hebrew word, zĕʿāqâ and ṣĕʿāqâ; both are translated as "cry" or "outcry."

ease, but did not aid the poor and needy. They were haughty and did an abomination before me. So I removed them, when I saw it.

— Ezekiel 16:48–50

The word "abomination" (*to'ebah*) sounds like the language of Leviticus (18:22; 20:13), which forbade a man to lie with another man, but "abomination" is used to describe many other things: idolatry (Deut. 7:26), non-kosher diets (Deut. 14:3), improper sacrifices (Prov. 21:27; Isa. 1:13). In the immediate context of Ezekiel, "abomination" involved injustice and adultery (Ezek. 18:12; 22:11; 33:26).

While sexual behavior might be behind some of Ezekiel's language, the sin of injustice comes out more clearly. Sodom was prosperous and lazy; they didn't aid the poor and needy; they had too much food. (Does that sound like any country you know?) To summarize, Sodom was not hospitable. Ezekiel helps explain why Sodom's victims were crying out: they were hungry, poor, and needy but received no hospitality from Sodom. Sodom was guilty of injustice and inhospitality.

However, the first sin mentioned in Ezekiel's list isn't one of these but pride. Ezekiel also says they were haughty, which sounds like pride. If the big sin of Sodom was pride, I guess that means anyone who struggles with pride is guilty of Sodomy. According to Ezekiel 16, I'm a Sodomite. And you probably are too. (You may not want to admit that in church.)

Isaiah and Ezekiel, therefore, support the idea in Genesis 19 that Sodom was guilty of inhospitality and injustice, and Ezekiel adds pride. Why is Ezekiel 16's perspective of Sodom ignored in the church? It's easier to focus on other people's problems and not our own. Some of the most vocal critics in the church of homosexual behavior seem to be guilty of pride, which makes them Sodomites too, like you and me. As we move to the New Testament, we'll see that Jesus didn't just accuse people of being Sodomites; he said they were worse than Sodomites.

Jesus: Cities Worse Than Sodom

Jesus in the Gospels, like me in *God Behaving Badly*, avoids the topic of homosexuality, but also like me in this book, he doesn't ignore the city of Sodom. (Unfortunately, that's where the similarities end.) While Noah, the hero of God's first major destruction, appears eight times in the New Testament,[20] Sodom, the target of the second destruction, appears nine times.[21] And interestingly, all five of the gospel occurrences of Sodom come from the mouth of Jesus.

How does Jesus speak of the city destroyed by fire and brimstone? Unlike the WBC, he never says God hates Sodomites, and he never associates the city with sexual immorality. Shortly after connecting Sodom to the sin of inhospitality (Matt. 10:13–15), Jesus mentions Sodom twice in comparisons to Galilean cities (Matt. 11:20–24).

> And if the house is worthy, let your peace come upon it, but if it is not worthy, let your peace return to you. And if anyone will not receive you or listen to your words, shake off the dust from your feet when you leave that house or town. Truly, I say to you, it will be more bearable on the day of judgment for the land of **Sodom** and Gomorrah than for that *town*. ...
>
> Then he began to denounce the cities where most of his mighty works had been done, because they did not repent. "**Woe to you**, Chorazin! **Woe to you**, Bethsaida! For if the mighty works done in you had been done in Tyre and Sidon, they would have repented long ago in sackcloth and ashes. But I tell you, it will be more bearable on the day of judgment for Tyre and Sidon than for you.
>
> And you, Capernaum, will you be exalted to heaven?
>
> You will be brought down to Hades.
>
> For if the mighty works done in you had been done in

---

20. New Testament references for Noah: Matthew 24:37–38; Luke 3:36; 17:26–27; Hebrews 11:7; 1 Peter 3:20; 2 Peter 2:5.

21. New Testament references for Sodom: Matthew 10:15; 11:23–24; Luke 10:12; 17:29; Romans 9:29; 2 Peter 2:6; Jude 1:7; Revelation 11:8.

> **Sodom**, it would have remained until this day. But I tell you
> that it will be more tolerable on the day of judgment for the
> land of **Sodom** than for you."
>
> — Matthew 10:13–15; 11:20–24

Jesus' language seems harsh; we prefer what he says just a few verses later (Matt. 11:28, "Come to me all who labor and are heavy-laden …"), but he often used provocative language to get people's attention.

Whose attention is Jesus trying to get here? Israelites, but not just Israelites; Galileans, but not just Galileans. The three Galilean cities he mentions (Chorazin, Bethsaida, and Capernaum) are all on the north shore of the sea of Galilee, an area very familiar to Jesus. They were his neighbors. The city of Capernaum was his home during his ministry (Matt. 4:13). Jesus knew this region of Galilee better than any other, and they knew Jesus. They would not have considered themselves bad people, certainly not like Sodom. For us today, rough equivalents to Jesus' audience would not be people from a different country, from a different denomination, or with a different sexual preference, but people from our own country, our own denomination, even our own church. How long would pastors last if they called people in their church Sodomites or said they were worse than Sodom? Perhaps followers of Jesus should follow Jesus' example and save our strongest rhetoric not for strangers or people outside the church but for those closest to us.

What was Jesus' message for his "fellow parishioners"? In a word, "Woe!" While the word has disappeared from our vernacular, you know you don't want someone to say "woe" to you. Woe is a word of warning. Jesus is telling these Galilean Jews that as wicked as Sodom was, they are worse because they have seen Jesus' acts of power but are still unrepentant. If Sodom had seen what they had seen, even that wicked city would have repented. Jesus is saying to these cities not, "You're like Sodom," but, "You're worse than Sodom."

Notice that both Jesus and WBC use provocative language to get one's attention. What's the difference between Jesus' "Worse than Sodom" campaign and the WBC's "God hates fags" campaign? Aren't both messages equally insulting?

It's the difference between love and hate. WBC may be involved in ministries of compassion to the LGBT community (I doubt it), but their message is focused on divine hatred. Earlier in Matthew's gospel, Jesus had been teaching, serving, and healing his Galilean neighbors before he issued this warning to them.[22] His shocking warning was a continuation of his ministry of compassion and love.

Before destroying the city, God warned Sodom. And then Sodom itself became a symbol of warning used by the prophets in the Old Testament and by Jesus in the New Testament to get the attention of the Israelites in an attempt to provoke them to repent.

As we attempt to follow the examples of the prophets and Jesus, who should we be warning? Based on what we've seen in this chapter, prime candidates for warnings include anyone involved in non-ideal sexual relationships, anyone who practices inhospitality, anyone not involved in justice, anyone not caring for the poor, anyone who is proud.

But before warning Sodom, God showed compassion on them, and before warning these Galileans, Jesus showed compassion on them. So before warning someone, ask yourself a few questions.

- Am I praying for them?
- Am I acting like Abraham — delivering, interceding, and risking my life for them?
- Am I acting like Jesus — teaching, serving, and healing them?

And remember that even after we've served, healed, and loved, the people we warn may still choose to ignore our words, so we'll need to keep praying.

Gary

Gary was one of my most significant spiritual mentors. I met him my first year in college. He challenged me, encouraged me, and helped me discern my call to Christian ministry as I came on staff with IVCF.

---

22. Here are references in Matthew's gospel of Jesus' ministry to these Galileans before he compared them to Sodom: teaching (Matt. 5–7), serving (Matt. 8:23–27), and healing (Matt. 4:23–24; 8:1–17, 28–33; 9:2–8, 18–34).

Gary trained me as a Bible teacher and speaker. While I was on staff at his alma mater, he supported my ministry. In 1991, after giving Shannon and me marital counseling, Gary spoke at our wedding.

About six years ago, Gary announced that he was gay and that he had decided to pursue a homosexual lifestyle.

What do you do when the person who performed your wedding and gave you advice about marriage takes such a dramatic step away from what you believe to be the biblical ideal of marriage? I was stunned, as were many of my Christian friends who knew him, were influenced by him, or had their weddings performed by him.

I wasn't sure what to do about my friendship with Gary, so I just ignored him, and I suspect many of my other friends simply did the same. My family didn't live on the same coast of the United States, so avoidance was easy for us, but when we traveled to the other coast, we didn't go out of our way to see Gary.

On a recent trip to California, as I was staying with my brother's family, Rich informed me that he had invited Gary over for dessert. He asked, "Is that okay?" I hadn't seen Gary since his announcement. My response was less than enthusiastic. "Sure. That's fine." I didn't really feel like being hospitable, and I was a bit apprehensive about our time together. Would it be awkward? If the topic of his lifestyle came up, what would I say? What should I say?

My concerns turned out to be unwarranted. The evening was enjoyable and entertaining. I didn't bring up Leviticus 18, Genesis 19, or goat-boiling, and I think that was the right choice.

I later discovered that Rich, unlike me, had continued to take initiative with Gary even after his big announcement. Rich decided to keep pursuing his friendship with Gary even as Gary seemed to be moving away from historic Christianity. As I think of Rich's concern for Gary, it reminds me of Abraham's concern for the people of Sodom, God's concern for the victims of Sodom, and Jesus' concern for his Galilean neighbors. And it reminds me to pray for my friends like Gary.

EPILOGUE
Sex and the Single Savior

We arrived fifteen minutes early, but the room was already packed. The capacity was three hundred, but there were far more than that in the room. People were in the aisles; they were sitting on each others' laps. The room buzzed with anticipation. No sycamore-tree-climbing tax collectors yet, but they would probably be arriving soon.

Fortunately, I was one of the two speakers. For the first time in my life I felt like a celebrity. People called out, "Make room for the speaker." The sea parted as my friend Barb and I made our way to the front of the room.

Were they there to hear us? No. While it would have been nice to think otherwise, the throngs weren't there because of the speakers. The draw was the topic.

We were at the Urbana Missions Conference in December 1996, where twenty thousand college students gathered from around the world to learn about God's mission for the planet.[1] Barb and I were leading the seminar on "Romantic Relationships." It might not have been a popular topic among lightsaber-wielding boys, or among cane-wielding geriatrics, but to get into the room that day, these eighteen- to twenty-two-year-olds would have cut holes in the ceiling.

---

1. The Urbana conference is sponsored by InterVarsity Christian Fellowship. For more information, see *https://urbana.org/*.

They may, however, have been disappointed with our message, which was essentially, "Fall in love with Jesus first."

Fall in Love with Jesus First

As we discussed in chapter 1, our culture is obsessed with sex. It's everywhere: films, TV, billboards, books, magazines, even beer commercials. The church, however, often ignores the topic. We don't feel comfortable talking about sex in church, and we avoid the sexual scandals of the Bible.

The church is obsessed not with sex but with marriage. In the church, we frequently celebrate marriage (which is great), but we rarely celebrate singleness (which is not great). Since many events are focused on meeting the needs of couples and families, single people in the church often feel ignored, avoided, and even ostracized.[2]

The crazy crowds at the Urbana Romantic Relationships seminar weren't there because of the speakers, but they wanted to hear about the topic in order to take the next step in their inevitable march toward marriage. They would have climbed trees and ripped holes in ceilings to avoid the gift of singleness, which they viewed as more of a curse. Marriage was deemed essential for future happiness. But anything other than God that makes such a bold claim on our allegiance is an idol.

In chapter 2, we discussed how sex and marriage are gifts from God. The appropriate response to receiving a gift is to thank the giver. But from the beginning, we humans have had a problem taking God's gifts and focusing exclusively on them, even to the point of worshiping them (the fruit, the helper, the sex, and the children). When humans worship these gifts, and not the God who gave them, the Bible calls it

---

2. For an excellent discussion of this topic, see Albert Y. Hsu, *Singles at the Crossroads: A Fresh Perspective on Christian Singleness* (Downers Grove, Ill.: InterVarsity, 1997). The interview with John Stott (1921–2011), who lived a celibate life, is particularly insightful. See also the website of Wesley Hill and Ron Belgau: *http://spiritualfriendship.org.*

idolatry. Our culture makes sex into an idol, and the church makes marriage into an idol.

What does the Bible tell us to do with idols? To defame them.[3] Tear them down and show that they are not worthy of worship. Only one object in the cosmos deserves our worship: God. That's why we told the hordes at the Romantic Relationship seminar to "fall in love with Jesus first." Not surprisingly, Jesus' life and ministry appropriately defame the idols of sex and marriage, so let's go there next.

Jesus' Scandalous Family

Many people like to research their genealogy to discover their roots, which can often be a source of pride as they discover famous ancestors. As we've researched the people in Jesus' genealogy (Matthew 1) to discover his roots, we've realized that many of his ancestors weren't really people one would brag about.

- *Abraham* was an incestuous pimping polygamous patriarch and his sister/wife *Sarah* appears to have been a victim of a power rape by Pharaoh of Egypt (see chapters 2 through 6).
- Their grandson *Jacob* was an incestuous polygamist, not because he married his cousins (that was okay back then) but because he married two sisters, *Leah* and Rachel (see chapters 3 and 6).
- The son of Jacob and Leah, *Judah* visited a hooker, who just happened to be his daughter-in law, *Tamar,* the pious prostitute (see chapter 4).
- Their descendant, *Salmon,* married *Rahab* the faithful prostitute (see chapter 4).
- Their son, *Boaz,* married *Ruth,* whose incester ancestor, *Moab,* was the son — and grandson — of Lot, nephew of

---

3. Notable Old Testament examples of idol defaming are performed by Gideon (Judg. 6:25–32), Elijah (1 Kings 18:20–40), Jehu (2 Kings 10:18–27), Hezekiah (2 Kings 18:4), and Josiah (2 Kings 23:15–20).

Abraham, and resident of Sodom, so technically, a Sodomite (see chapters 6 and 7).

- The great-grandson of Boaz and Ruth, *David*, was a polygamous rapist (after God's own heart?), and his wife, *Bathsheba*, was a power rape victim (see chapters 3 and 5).
- Their son, *Solomon*, somehow managed to build a temple while maintaining a harem of seven hundred wives and three hundred concubines (see chapter 3).

Jesus had a shockingly scandalous ancestry. Prostitutes and polygamists, rapists and adulterers, incesters and Sodomites. Love, Old Testament style. All in Jesus' family tree.

The problems continue as we look at Jesus' immediate family. While Christians believe Jesus was born of the Virgin Mary and conceived by the Holy Spirit, I doubt his neighbors shared this belief. To people who were familiar with the situation, it would appear that Jesus was conceived out of wedlock, and thus he was an illegitimate child.

Jesus' family tree was not characterized by a series of perfect marriages, and yet it culminated in the birth of God's Son, the only totally holy human. What can we learn from Jesus' family? Two lessons.

First, don't idolize marriage. As we can see from these many examples from Jesus' family, marriages often were not ideal. They had problems back then just as they do today. The Bible defames the idol of marriage, not by covering up but by exposing all the ways it can go wrong. If the church talks about marriage only in idyllic terms, then those of us who struggle in our marriages could feel like we have no place in the church. Marriage is a gift from God, but not something to be worshiped. God is the only object worthy of worship.

Second, don't ignore the stories of sex scandals in Scripture. You should probably avoid participating in sex scandals, but when they take place, talk about them. The Bible, particularly the Old Testament, doesn't ignore them. Scripture includes these stories and even highlights them in Jesus' genealogy. If the church were to spend more time teaching about and learning from these non-ideal sexual situations, there would be fewer sex scandals in the church. When Paul says all

Scripture is inspired and profitable for teaching, he says nothing about excluding the stories of Abraham, the pimping patriarch, and David, the polygamous rapist. By teaching on these stories, we reveal an amazingly gracious God who not only can forgive scandalous sexual sins but also can work powerfully to accomplish his purposes through seriously flawed sinners. After all, love, Old Testament style, and love, New Testament style, are not primarily about human love but are about divine love. It's a love story between a merciful God and sinful humans.

Sex and the Single Savior

In earlier chapters, we looked at Jesus' attitudes toward polygamists, prostitutes, adulterers, and Sodomites; now let's see what he says directly about marriage. To begin with, we should note that Jesus didn't talk about marriage much. Unlike many pastors and ministers today, Jesus never taught a romantic relationships seminar, he never did marital counseling, and he never performed a wedding. (Although, he did provide a lot of liquor for one; John 2:1–11.) The fact that Jesus didn't focus much attention on marriage should be a warning to his followers not to be obsessed with the institution. When Jesus did speak about marriage, his message was not only surprising but also defaming of marriage as an idol in two ways.

First, as we already observed in chapter 3, Jesus taught that people won't be married in heaven. In the context of the Sadducees' outrageous question about one bride for seven brothers, Jesus informs them,

> When they rise from the dead, they neither marry nor
> are given in marriage, but are like angels in heaven.
> — Mark 12:25

Thinking about this teaching for long makes me really sad, because I would love to be in full partnership with my wife, Shannon, forever. But then I am consoled as I consider that the communion with Jesus will somehow be even better. As wonderful and as important as my relationship with my spouse is, it is still relatively short-lived in comparison with my eternal relationship with God.

Second, Jesus taught that for some people, it would be better for them to stay single. When the Pharisees asked him about divorce (Matt. 19:3–6), Jesus replied that what God has brought together (Gen. 2:24), humans should not separate, which surprised the disciples and prompted this interaction.

> The disciples said to him, "If such is the case of a man with his **wife**, it is better not to **marry**." But he said to them, "Not everyone can receive this saying, but only those to whom it is given. For there are **eunuchs** who have been so from birth, and there are **eunuchs** who have been made **eunuchs** by men, and there are **eunuchs** who have made themselves **eunuchs** for the sake of the kingdom of heaven. Let the one who is able to receive this receive it."
>
> —Matthew 19:10–12

Jesus' language here is a bit confusing as he speaks of three types of eunuchs: (1) men who were born without the ability to be sexually active; (2) men who were castrated later in life, typically to serve as keepers of a royal harem (2 Kings 20:18; Est. 2:14); (3) men who choose to live a celibate lifestyle to serve God better. The word *eunuch* technically refers to the second group only, but Jesus uses it figuratively to refer to voluntary abstinence in the case of the third group.

While Jesus' words might seem confusing, the disciples' initial comment is clearly about people deciding not to get married. Jesus then speaks about a celibate lifestyle as a gift ("to whom it is given"), and he recommends receiving it if possible ("Let the one who is able to receive this receive it.") Some readers may feel a bit uncomfortable with this teaching of Jesus, since it gets ignored by most Bible teachers, but Paul says something similar to the Corinthians when he recommends that unmarried people stay unmarried (1 Cor. 7:7–8).

And before we go any farther, can we think of any examples of important people in the New Testament who chose a lifestyle of celibacy? Hmm, let's see. There's Paul (1 Cor. 7:8).[4] Anyone else? Ah, yes — Jesus.

---

4. Some scholars think Paul may have been married but was a widower when he wrote

It is shocking that the two most significant individuals in the New Testament both chose to remain single to serve God better.[5] In our teaching about Christian marriage, how could we have ignored the celibate examples of Paul and Jesus? Because the church tends to make marriage into an idol.

Ironically, Jesus' single status would make him not welcome in many Christian events today.[6] As a single male in his thirties, he couldn't participate in a couples' small group. He probably wouldn't be invited to be the speaker at family camp and perhaps not even asked to be a volunteer worker in the nursery.

Don't get me wrong; I'm not recommending that most Christians remain single (I love being married to Shannon); I'm simply saying that marriage as an idol should be defamed so that people who choose for one reason or another to live a single life, like Jesus and Paul, don't feel ostracized within the confines of the church.[7] Singles should not feel excluded among a group of people who are following a single Savior.

But Jesus Is the Bridegroom

Jesus didn't talk about marriage much, but he did have a habit of calling himself a bridegroom (Matt. 9:15; 25:1, 5–6, 10; Mark 2:19–20; Luke 5:34–35). And John the Baptist also called him the bridegroom (John 3:29). Jesus was a single savior, but he also had a spouse. Huh?

If Jesus is the bridegroom, who is the bride? His bride is his church, his followers. Now, some men may have trouble thinking of themselves as a bride, but they'll just need to get used to the idea. ("Woman up,"

---

1 Corinthians. See the blog of Denny Burke on this topic: *http://www.dennyburk.com/was-the-apostle-paul-married/*.

5. Unfortunately, the Protestant church has almost no models of leaders who chose a celibate lifestyle (except for John Stott), and tragically, the Catholic church has had serious sex scandals among its "celibate" clergy.

6. I am speaking more pointedly toward my own church context as a Protestant. See also the previous note.

7. For an honest, engaging story of a gay Christian who chose to lead a celibate lifestyle, see Wesley Hill, *Washed and Waiting: Reflections on Christian Faithfulness and Homosexuality* (Grand Rapids, Mich.: Zondervan, 2010).

guys!) We don't have to wear a white dress; it requires more than a change of clothes. As his bride, we will need to devote our lives fully to serving and following him. While all Christians are married to Jesus, it's a little more straightforward for the ones who are celibate since there's no slightly polygamous loyalty problem arising from trying to please multiple spouses. As anyone who is married knows, every marriage has problems.

Marriage appears as a metaphor throughout Scripture, but unfortunately the relationship between God and humans was often far from ideal. The text frequently describes Israel's sin and idolatry as sexual infidelity (Exod. 34:15–16; Lev. 17:7; 20:6; Num. 15:39; Deut. 31:16; 2 Chron. 21:11, 13; Jer. 2:20; 3:1, 3; Ezek. 16:15, 30–35; 23:7, 19, 43–44; Hos. 3:3; 9:1). In the Old Testament, God's people had serious problems keeping up their side of the marital agreement. Which is why it's important to make our relationship with God the highest priority, even above our relationship with our spouse. Before entering into a romantic relationship, fall in love with Jesus first. If you end up together, your marriage will be stronger because you both love Jesus.

My Worst Sin

From age fourteen to twenty, I went through a series of girlfriends, most of which lasted no more than a few months. Many of them dropped me, eventually dropping the f-bomb. ("Let's just be *friends*.") The three Marys were the most problematic, since it didn't take a genius to figure out a taunt linking Mary with a guy named Lamb.

As a sophomore in college, I met Katherine, who was a freshman, as we were both involved with Stanford Christian Fellowship, but we didn't really become friends until the following year. I was attracted to her for a variety of reasons. She was beautiful. She had a great sense of humor. (At least, she laughed at my jokes.) I was in a fraternity and she was in a sorority. We were pursuing the same major and were both from the Midwest. And she was a Christian. *A gift from the Lord!*

But since I was never very good at taking initiative with members of the female sex, it is unlikely anything would have developed between us, until I was assigned to work with the small group Bible study she was leading. I was a junior experienced leader, and she was a sophomore leading for the first time. In the context of our fellowship, I was her spiritual supervisor. That wasn't my decision, and it may have been a bad one, but I wasn't going to complain. Katherine and I started dating early that fall.

The relationship started out great. Since we had the same major, we had classes together. I gave her feedback on her small group. We became deeper friends. But gradually we became more involved physically, and it became a serious problem. We never had sex, but it was close.

One afternoon, my InterVarsity staff worker, Bill, asked to meet with me. After chatting for a few minutes, he asked, "How are things going with Katherine?"

I said, "Fine." Which was a lie.

Bill persisted. "How are things going in your physical relationship?"

I responded, "Fine." Another lie.

He asked, "What do you mean, 'Fine'?"

"Bill, that's none of your business."

When someone tells you it's none of your business, it still might be your business. (What would have happened if David said to Nathan, "It's none of your business"?) Bill got serious, "Are you having sex?"

I thought, "Oh, crap, I think he suspects something." I paused, a long pause, perhaps too long of a pause. "No."

"What are you doing physically?"

I thought, "Wow, he's not going to leave me alone." I finally decided I should tell him, so I confessed to Bill about our overly physical relationship.

He was gracious but firm. "Dave, you're supposed to be caring for her spiritually, not lusting after her sexually. I think you guys need to break up." I knew he was right. I hope you have friends in your life like Bill.

It was very difficult for both of us to end the relationship. It's always painful to get rid of an idol. Katherine wasn't the idol, but it was the relationship that was taking me away from God and community.

I began this book by sharing an unfinished story about an awkward experience of being asked the question, "What was the worst sin you've ever committed?" You might think it would have been tough to decide because I had so many options to choose from, but my relationship with Katherine was the first thing that came to mind that day. I talked about my lust, my deception to Bill, and my exploiting of a relationship where I was supposed to be a servant leader. Fortunately, I follow a single Savior who came to seek and to save the lost and to forgive sinful people like me.

Seven Years of Singleness

Prior to Katherine, I had been in eight romantic relationships over the course of the previous six years. But at that point in my life I felt like God was telling me to take a break. I needed to take a serious step away from this particular idol in order to properly defame it and work on my relationship with God. I told Bill and several other friends about my decision, because I knew that telling others would make it more real.

While I initially envisioned a break from dating of two years, two became three, then four, five, six, and seven. I didn't date from age twenty to twenty-eight. After my series of relationships, seven and a half years felt like a very long time. That's a difficult time in one's life to be single. It seemed like everyone else was moving toward marriage. During that period, there were several women I was interested in romantically, but I knew it was better for my soul not to date and be faithful to my commitment to take a break. It was costly, particularly when I felt lonely, when women I liked moved into relationships with other guys, and as I frequently attended the weddings of close friends and ex-girlfriends. It was painful, brutal, and costly.

Costly, but worth it.

After I graduated, I came on staff with InterVarsity to do campus ministry. Since I was single, I was able to give myself wholeheartedly to college students. I ate most of my meals with them and went on numerous road trips with them. I participated in summer missions programs with ministry partners, traveling to northern Nigeria, to the Yucatan peninsula of Mexico, and to inner-city Newark, New Jersey. I twice took students with me evangelistic hitchhiking four hundred miles up the 5 freeway from Los Angeles to San Francisco. After arriving in the Bay Area, I did open-air preaching with students on Sproul Plaza on the University of California Berkeley campus. I took students with me to visit the AIDS wing of the Chino prison, where we prayed and worshiped with inmates.

Those years were times of deep spiritual growth and maturity for me. I read about the life of St. Francis, a celibate monk who committed his life to following Jesus and caring for the poor. I spent time studying the Bible and slowly started to discern a new call from God on my life, to focus on teaching the Bible, since I loved to give others a love of God's Word. Over the course of those seven and a half years of singleness, I also fell more deeply in love with Jesus.

When God finally woke me up and brought Shannon into my life, I was ready for marriage. ("Bone of my bone, flesh of my flesh …") It was definitely worth the wait. Shannon was a ministry partner. She helped me be a better servant of Jesus and others. I loved her and she loved me. But, and here's the crucial piece, we both loved Jesus more.

The Marriage of the Lamb

For our wedding, we included a verse in the invitation that we sent out to our friends, which hopefully you won't find irreverent.

> Blessed are those who are invited to the marriage supper
> of the Lamb.
>
> — Revelation 19:9

While we hope that we were somehow able to bless the four hundred or so people who came to our wedding, all of us, married and single, are invited to the ultimate marriage supper of Jesus, the true Lamb of God, where we'll be blessed beyond belief as we

> rejoice and exult
> > and give him the glory,
> for the marriage of the Lamb has come,
> and his Bride has made herself ready.

> — Revelation 19:7

Amen. Now, let's get ready to worship the bridegroom.

BIBLIOGRAPHY

Abasili, Alexander Izuchukwu. "Was It Rape? The David and Bathsheba Pericope Re-Examined." *Vetus Testamentum* 61 (2011): 1–15.

Alexander, T. Desmond, and David Baker. *Dictionary of the Old Testament: Pentateuch.* Downers Grove, Ill.: InterVarsity, 2003.

Alter, Robert. *Ancient Israel: The Former Prophets: Joshua, Judges, Samuel and Kings.* New York: Norton, 2013.

———. *The Five Books of Moses: A Translation with Commentary.* New York: Norton, 2004.

Anderson, A. A. *2 Samuel.* Dallas: Word, 1989.

Arnold, Bill T., and H. G. M. Williamson. *Dictionary of the Old Testament: Historical Books.* Downers Grove, Ill.: InterVarsity, 2005.

Bailey, Kenneth E. *Jesus through Middle Eastern Eyes.* Downers Grove, Ill.: InterVarsity, 2008.

Baker, David L. *Tight Fists or Open Hands? Wealth and Poverty in Old Testament Law.* Grand Rapids, Mich.: Eerdmans, 2009.

Brown, Christa. *This Little Light: Beyond a Baptist Preacher Predator and His Gang.* Cedarburg, Wis.: Foremost, 2009.

Brown, F., S. Driver, and C. Briggs. *The Brown-Driver-Briggs Hebrew and English Lexicon.* 1906; Peabody, Mass.: Hendrickson, 1997.

Brownson, James V. *Bible, Gender, Sexuality: Reframing the Church's Debate on Same-Sex Relationships.* Grand Rapids, Mich.: Eerdmans, 2013.

Bruce, F. F. *The Gospel of John.* Grand Rapids, Mich.: Eerdmans, 1983.

Copan, Paul. *Is God a Moral Monster? Making Sense of the Old Testament.* Grand Rapids, Mich.: Baker, 2011.

Creach, Jerome F. D. *Violence in Scripture.* Louisville: Westminster John Knox, 2013.

Davidson, Richard M. "Did David Rape Bathsheba? A Case Study in Narrative Theology." *Journal of the Adventist Theological Society* 17 (2006): 81–95.

Evans, Rachel Held. *A Year of Biblical Womanhood*. Nashville: Thomas Nelson, 2012.

Firth, David G. *1 and 2 Samuel*. Downers Grove, Ill.: InterVarsity, 2009.

Gitari, David. "The Church and Polygamy." *Transformation* 1 (1984): 3–10.

Goldingay, John. *Men Behaving Badly*. Carlisle, UK: Paternoster, 2000.

Gordon, Robert P. *I and II Samuel: A Commentary*. Waynesboro, Ga.: Paternoster, 1986.

Grudem, Wayne. *Evangelical Feminism and Biblical Truth*. Sisters, Ore.: Multnomah, 2004.

Haugen, Gary. *Just Courage: God's Great Expedition for the Restless Christian*. Downers Grove, Ill.: InterVarsity, 2008.

Higgs, Liz Curtis. *Bad Girls of the Bible: And What We Can Learn from Them*. Colorado Springs: WaterBrook, 1999.

———. *Really Bad Girls of the Bible: More Lessons from Less-Than-Perfect Women*. Colorado Springs: WaterBrook, 2000.

Hill, Wesley. *Washed and Waiting: Reflections on Christian Faithfulness and Homosexuality*. Grand Rapids, Mich.: Zondervan, 2010.

Hsu, Albert Y. *Singles at the Crossroads: A Fresh Perspective on Christian Singleness*. Downers Grove, Ill.: InterVarsity, 1997.

James, Carolyn Custis. *The Gospel of Ruth: Loving God Enough to Break the Rules*. Grand Rapids, Mich.: Zondervan, 2008.

———. *Lost Women of the Bible: The Women We Thought We Knew*. Grand Rapids, Mich.: Zondervan, 2005.

Kidner, Derek. *Genesis*. Downers Grove, Ill.: InterVarsity, 1967.

Kinnaman, David, and Gabe Lyons. *Unchristian: What a New Generation Really Thinks about Christianity ... and Why It Matters*. Grand Rapids, Mich.: Baker, 2007.

Koenig, Sara M. *Isn't This Bathsheba?* Eugene, Ore.: Pickwick, 2011.

Kristof, Nicholas D., and Sheryl WuDunn. *Half the Sky: Turning Oppression into Opportunities for Women Worldwide*. New York: Knopf, 2009.

Lamb, David T. *God Behaving Badly: Is the God of the Old Testament Angry, Sexist, and Racist?* Downers Grove, Ill.: InterVarsity, 2011.

———. *Righteous Jehu and His Evil Heirs: The Deuteronomist's Negative Perspective on Dynastic Succession*. Oxford: Oxford Univ. Press, 2007.

———. "Trash Talking, Derogatory Rhetoric and Psychological Warfare in Ancient Israel." In *Warfare, Ritual, and Symbol in Biblical and Modern Contexts*, edited by B. E. Kelle, F. R. Ames, and J. L. Wright, 111–30. Atlanta: Society of Biblical Literature, 2014.

Langberg, Diane Mandt. *Counseling Survivors of Sexual Abuse*. Maitland, Fla.: Xulon Press, 2003.

———. *On the Threshold of Hope: Opening the Door to Healing for Survivors of Sexual Abuse*. Wheaton, Ill.: Tyndale, 1999.

Loader, William. *Making Sense of Sex: Attitudes towards Sexuality in Early Jewish and Christian Literature*. Grand Rapids, Mich.: Eerdmans, 2013.

Marin, Andrew. *Love Is an Orientation: Elevating the Conversation with the Gay Community*. Downers Grove, Ill.: InterVarsity, 2009.

Nichol, George G. "The Alleged Rape of Bathsheba: Some Observations on Ambiguity in Biblical Narrative." *Journal for the Study of the Old Testament* 73 (1997): 43–54.

Richards, E. Randolph, and Brandon J. O'Brien. *Misreading Scripture with Western Eyes: Removing Cultural Blinders to Better Understand the Bible*. Downers Grove, Ill.: InterVarsity, 2012.

Seibert, Eric. *The Violence of Scripture: Overcoming the Old Testament's Troubling Legacy*. Minneapolis: Fortress, 2012.

Smith, Brendan Powell. *The Brick Bible: A New Spin on the Old Testament*. New York: Skyhorse, 2011.

Tigay, Jeffrey H. *Deuteronomy*. Philadelphia: Jewish Publication Society, 1996.

Trible, Phyllis. *Texts of Terror: Literary-Feminist Readings of Biblical Narratives*. Philadelphia: Fortress, 1984.

Vines, Matthew. *God and the Gay Christian: The Biblical Case in Support of Same-Sex Relationships*. Colorado Springs: Convergent, 2014.

Ward, Benedicta. *Harlots of the Desert: A Study of Repentance in Early Monastic Sources*. Kalamazoo, Mich.: Cistercian, 1987.

Webb, William. *Slaves, Women, and Homosexuals*. Downers Grove, Ill.: InterVarsity, 2001.

Wenham, Gordon J. *The Book of Leviticus*. Grand Rapids, Mich.: Eerdmans, 1979.

———. *Genesis 1–15, Genesis 16–50*. Waco, Dallas: Word, 1987, 1994.

———. *Numbers: An Introduction and Commentary*. Downers Grove, Ill.: InterVarsity, 1981.

Wright, Christopher J. H. *Deuteronomy*. Peabody, Mass.: Hendrickson, 2003.

———. *Old Testament Ethics for the People of God*. Downers Grove, Ill.: InterVarsity, 2004.

Yarhouse, Mark. *Homosexuality and the Christian: A Guide for Parents, Pastors, and Friends*. Bloomington, Minn.: Bethany, 2010.

SCRIPTURE INDEX